Frommer's™

Budapest
day BY day™

1st Edition

by Robert Smyth

WILEY

A John Wiley and Sons, Ltd, Publication

Contents

UK Publisher: Sally Smith
Executive Project Editor: Daniel Mersey
Commissioning Editor: Fiona Quinn
Development Editor: Karen Fitzpatrick
Content Editor: Erica Peters
Cartography: SY Cartographics
Photo Research: Jill Emeny

Wiley also publishes its books in a variety of electronic formats. Some
content that appears in print may not be available in electronic books.

British Library Cataloguing in Publication Data

A catalogue record for this book is available from the British Library

ISBN: 978-0-470-69758-0

Typeset by Wiley Indianapolis Composition Services

Printed and bound in China by RR Donnelley

5 4 3 2 1

A Note from the Editorial Director

Organizing your time. That's what this guide is all about.

Other guides give you long lists of things to see and do and then expect you to fit the pieces together. The Day by Day guides are different. These guides tell you the best of everything, and then they show you how to see it *in the smartest, most time-efficient way*. Our authors have designed detailed itineraries organized by time, neighborhood, or special interest. And each tour comes with a bulleted map that takes you from stop to stop.

Hoping to tour the best in Habsburg and art nouveau 'szecesszio' architecture as well as see what traces the communists and Turks left behind? Looking to taste your way through Budapest's burgeoning restaurant scene, sample Hungary's fine wines and hang out at the city's hippest nightspots? Whatever your interest or schedule, the Day by Days give you the smartest routes to follow. Not only do we take you to the top attractions, hotels, and restaurants, but we also help you access those special moments that locals get to experience—those 'finds' that turn tourists into travelers.

The Day by Days are also your top choice if you're looking for one complete guide for all your travel needs. The best hotels and restaurants for every budget, the greatest shopping values, the wildest nightlife—it's all here.

Why should you trust our judgment? Because our authors personally visit each place they write about. They're an independent lot who say what they think and would never include places they wouldn't recommend to their best friends. They're also open to suggestions from readers. If you'd like to contact them, please send your comments our way at feedback@frommers.com, and we'll pass them on.

Enjoy your Day by Day guide—the most helpful travel companion you can buy. And have the trip of a lifetime.

Warm regards,

Kelly Regan

Kelly Regan, Editorial Director
Frommer's Travel Guides

About the Author

Robert Smyth is a Budapest-based British journalist who hails from the River Mersey directly across from Liverpool. He has been living in Budapest for around 15 years during which time he's seen certain aspects of the city change beyond recognition, but can still find enough old world and quirky charm to keep him there. He holds a degree in Economics from the UK, which he followed up with an MBA at Budapest's former Karl Marx University only to find that writing holds more appeal than the world of business. He has written print and online guides respectively for the Blue Guides and Whatsonwhen; he also writes columns on wine tasting for the local English-language press and is *Business New Europe's* correspondent for Hungary. When not writing about traveling or wine, he likes to travel and taste wine.

Acknowledgments

For my partner Ágnes Molnár, our son Alex, my mother Sylvia and late father Robert Snr.

I'd like to give a big thanks to the Molnár family for their ongoing support throughout, photographer Bianca Otero and the Frommer's UK editorial team, the former with whom it was a pleasure to work with once again and the latter for the first time. Many thanks to all of you who have accompanied me on the great adventure that has been Budapest during the last 15 years. From drinking with me in the dingiest of wine bars to devouring goose liver in the finest restaurants, you're too many to mention but you know who you are.

An Additional Note

Please be advised that travel information is subject to change at any time—and this is especially true of prices. We therefore suggest that you write or call ahead for confirmation when making your travel plans. The authors, editors, and publisher cannot be held responsible for the experiences of readers while traveling. Your safety is important to us, however, so we encourage you to stay alert and be aware of your surroundings.

Star Ratings, Icons & Abbreviations

Every hotel, restaurant, and attraction listing in this guide has been ranked for quality, value, service, amenities, and special features using a **star-rating system.** Hotels, restaurants, attractions, shopping, and nightlife are rated on a scale of zero stars (recommended) to three stars (exceptional). In addition to the star-rating system, we also use a **kids icon** to point out the best bets for families. Within each tour, we recommend cafes, bars or restaurants where you can take a break. Each of these stops appears in a shaded box marked with a coffee cup–shaped bullet ☕.

The following **abbreviations** are used for credit cards:

AE	American Express	DISC	Discover	V	Visa
DC	Diners Club	MC	MasterCard		

Frommers.com

Now that you have this guidebook to help you plan a great trip, visit our website at **www.frommers.com** for additional travel information on more than 4,000 destinations. We update features regularly to give you instant access to the most current trip-planning information available. At Frommers.com, you'll find scoops on the best airfares, lodging rates, and car rental bargains. You can even book your travel online through our reliable travel booking partners. Other popular features include:

A Note on Prices

In the 'Take a Break' and 'Best Bets' sections of this book, we have used a system of dollar signs to show a range of costs for 1 night in a hotel (the price of a double-occupancy room) or the cost of an entree (main meal) at a restaurant. Use the following table to decipher the dollar signs:

Cost	Hotels	Restaurants
$	under $100	under $10
$$	$100–$200	$10–$20
$$$	$200–$300	$20–$30
$$$$	$300–$400	$30–$40
$$$$$	over $400	over $40

An Invitation to the Reader

In researching this book, we discovered many wonderful places—hotels, restaurants, shops, and more. We're sure you'll find others. Please tell us about them, so we can share the information with your fellow travelers in upcoming editions. If you were disappointed with a recommendation, we'd love to know that, too. Please write to:

Frommer's Budapest, Day by Day, 1st Edition
Wiley Publishing, Inc. • 111 River St. • Hoboken, NJ 07030-5774

15 Favorite
Moments

15 Favorite **Moments**

1. Great Market Hall
2. Gyul Baba utca
3. Széchenyi Baths
4. Budapest's Thermal Baths
5. View of Pest from Buda Palace
6. View from Margaret Island
7. Buda Palace
8. Rudás Baths
9. Statue Park
10. Budapest's Kert "Garden" Bars
11. Opera House
12. Museum Kávéház
13. Sziget Festival (Hajógyárisziget)
14. Castle District
15. Jewish District

Information
ⓜ Metro Station
Ⓗ HÉV Station
≋ Thermal Bath

0 ——— 1/2 mi
0 ——— 0.5 km

Budapest is a destination packed with impressive sights, including myriad buildings from the last great expansion phase of the Habsburg Empire, but many of my favorite moments are spent exploring the nooks and crannies that lie between the great edifices. From bathing in atmospheric thermal baths, drinking unique wines in funky bars in disused townhouse courtyards to exploring the city's Communist past, Budapest has many magic moments to savor.

1 Great Market Hall. I never get bored of taking the number 2 tram winding past Parliament, impressive waterfront buildings and down the river with the Castle District and Gellért Hill directly opposite on the way to buy 'Hungaricums' at the Great Market Hall. *See p 17.*

2 Gyül Baba utca. Being transported back to Turkish Budapest when climbing up the steep and narrow Gyul Baba utca, named after the dervish who brought the rose to Buda. Pay your respects at his tomb. *See p 31.*

3 Széchenyi Baths. Taking continental Europe's oldest underground that shunts under swish Andrássy út then soaking up the atmosphere at the neo-Baroque Széchenyi baths. *See p 13 & 27.*

4 Relaxing in the waters at any one of Budapest's classic thermal baths, switching between steaming hot and ice-cold pools, sauna, and steam and feeling as good as new. It's the ideal way to clear the cobwebs of the city's nightlife excesses. *See p 26.*

5 View of Pest from Buda Palace. Gazing down in amazement at buzzing Pest from the relative tranquility—depending on how many tourists are accompanying you—of the Buda Palace across the river. It's best in the morning as the city rolls into work opposite or lit up at night when the city folk start to play. *See p 61.*

6 Standing in the middle of the River Danube on Margaret Island and looking downstream to

Relaxing in the neo-Baroque Széchenyi baths.

The plush surroundings at the Opera House.

Parliament on one side and the Castle District on the other. Great for taking time out from the bustling city and enjoying a bit of green relief. *See p 88.*

7 **Buda Palace.** For a touch of refined hedonism, I enjoy mingling with the country's leading wine makers and drinking their fine wines in the splendor of Buda's Royal Palace—the best way to enjoy the castle. *See p 61.*

8 **Basking in the central pool at the Rudas Baths** with the sunlight beaming in through the cupola. *See p 27.*

9 **Contemplating the pillars of Communist society that once imposed themselves across the city but are now confined to the Statue Park,** part of the Memento Park. I find the replica of Stalin's boots, left behind when his statue was torn down at Felvonulási tér (Hungary's answer to Red Square), particularly significant. *See p 46.*

10 **Budapest's Kert 'Garden' Bars**. Feeling downright decadent—and very glad to live in Hungary after the winter is all but a memory—at one of the city's Kert 'Garden' summer bars. *See p 121.*

11 **Drinking bubbly on the balcony of the Opera House** during a break after marveling at the plush surroundings and wondering how the main chandelier can possibly stay up. *See p 8.*

12 **The tranquility of dawn and the power of the city's fin-de-siècle architecture from the terrace of the Museum Kávéház after a long night out.** There I love having one last Unicum and some pastry as the city starts to wake up.

13 **Sipping a beer while taking a ferry down the Danube to rock till I drop at the Sziget Festival,** and then hopping back on the ferry well after sunrise. *See p 161.*

14 **Exploring the old cobbled narrow streets of the Castle District** between Táncsics Mihály utca and Tóth Árpád sétány that are off the beaten track. *See p 60.*

15 **Feeling the buzz and ambience of the Jewish District**, which despite having seen a lot of adversity is still hanging on as buildings are bulldozed all around. *See p 54.* ●

1

The Best
Full-Day Tours

The Best **in One Day**

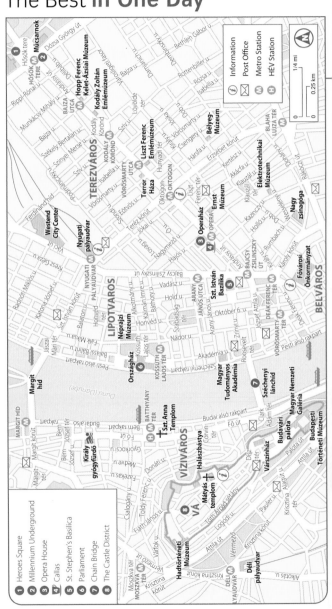

1 Heroes Square
2 Millennium Underground
3 Opera House
4 Callas
5 St. Stephen's Basilica
6 Parliament
7 Chain Bridge
8 The Castle District

Legend:
ⓘ Information
☒ Post Office
Ⓜ Metro Station
Ⓗ HÉV Station

0 — 0.25 km
0 — 1/4 mi

ere, I'm taking you on an action-packed tour that will leave you in awe of Budapest's architectural magnificence and magnitude. Particularly noteworthy is the architecture of the late 19th and early 20th centuries, when Hungary had finally found peace and prosperity. START: **Take the M1 Millennium Underground to Hősök tere.**

① ★★★ kids **Heroes Square (Hősök tere).** There's no better place to start getting your head around the turbulent history of Hungary than Heroes Square. The key protagonists are strikingly introduced as a series of imposing statues. The central column is guarded by the seven Magyar tribe leaders who, in 896AD, stormed into the Carpathian basin, comprising present-day Hungary and beyond. A statue of Árpád leads these seven heathen horsemen, and they appear to be kept in check by Archangel Gabriel, who presides over them from the top of the central column. The founding fathers are flanked by heroes including Szent (Saint) István, who converted Hungary to Christianity on Christmas Day in the year 1000AD, and all-conquering Kings Béla IV and Mátyás Corvinus, as well as perennial thorns in Habsburg Austria's side like Rákóczi and

Kossuth. Built in 1896 to celebrate a millennium of Magyar presence, nowadays Heroes Square is a popular place with skateboarders—oblivious to the significance of their country's heroes—and with right-wingers who use it as a backdrop for rallies. ⏱ *30 min. Hősök tere at crossing of Andrássy út and Dózsa György út. Metro: M1 to Hősök tere.*

② ★★ kids **Millennium Underground.** Take a ride on continental Europe's oldest metro, which opened in 1896 to coincide with the 1,000th anniversary of Magyar presence in Hungary. Get on at the Hősök tere stop and be whisked, just under street level, directly down the elegant Andrássy út (boulevard)—which I recommend you walk down on Day 2 (p 14, bullet **④**). Get off at Oktogon to see one of Budapest's several centers where Andrássy út meets the Nagy körút (the Great

The central column in Heroes Square is guarded by seven Magyar tribe leaders.

Take a ride on continental Europe's oldest metro.

Boulevard), or stay on one more stop to Opera. After London's underground system, this is the next oldest in the world and the stations in particular retain the fin-de-siècle feel. ⏱ *15 min. Entrance at end of Andrássy út at crossing of Andrássy út and Dózsa György út; on right-hand side of Andrássy út if looking from Heroes Square. First metro 4:36am, last 11:20pm. www.bkv.hu/metro/metro1.html. Single journey ticket Ft 270. Metro: M1 to Hősök tere.*

The Opera House.

❸ ★★★ **Opera House.** The Miklós Ybl-designed Opera House provides the sumptuous veneer to classy Andrássy út. If you can, I suggest you look now but come back and experience the Opera House in all its glory by catching a performance. Be warned that the super-steep cheap seats are not for sufferers of vertigo. The neo-Renaissance style of the exterior is all semi-circular arches and columns, and is symmetrically topped off by statues of idols of Hungarian opera, while statues of the two Hungarian musical greats, Liszt and Bartok, flank the main entrance. Step inside and the style changes dramatically to neo-classical with the walls and ceiling adorned by lavish works from leading Hungarian artists of the day, including Gyula Benczúr and Bertalan Székely. Exclusive Hungarian participation was deemed crucial in establishing the home of Hungarian opera, although the scary but magnificent-looking gold-plated, three-tonne chandelier was imported from Germany. ⏱ *15 min, 45 min if you take the tour, but check ahead as tours may be cancelled due to rehearsals. Andrássy út 22.*

☎ 153-0170 for tickets, 332-8197 for tours. www.opera.hu. Ft 2,600 (discount Ft 1,400). Tours at 3pm and 4pm daily, performances vary. Metro: M1 to Opera.

4 ★★ Callas. This, the former ticket office of the neighboring Opera, which can be viewed through the large arched windows, has been superbly spruced up by the noted British designer David Collins in an engaging blend of fin-de-siècle and Art Deco. While Callas is a serious dining venue with a decent sushi bar, it also does great Hungarian and international breakfasts, homemade pastries and cakes, as well as sandwiches. *Andrássy út 20.* ☎ *1/354-0954. $$.*

5 ★★★ St. Stephen's Basilica. Building this Budapest landmark proved a job too far for defining Hungarian architects József Hild and Miklós Ybl, who both died during the prolonged 54-year construction. The project literally hit rock bottom when the dome collapsed in 1868, a year after Hild's death. Architect József Kauser was called in and dragged Budapest's biggest church over the finishing line in 1905. A massive restoration project was completed in 2003 and the gleaming marble is the result of the application of 200kg of beeswax. Mathematically minded Hungarians love dealing in numbers and, like the Parliament's dome, Szent István's stands 96m/315ft high, as a tribute to the Magyar settlement of Hungary in 896. Had they arrived a few years earlier, perhaps the roof wouldn't have fallen in! The almost 1,000-year-old withered hand of St. Stephen, Hungary's first King, is displayed in the Szent Jobb Chapel. Another great Hungarian hero Ferenc Puskás, the talisman of the Magical Magyars and Real Madrid goal machine, was laid to rest here in 2006. An elevator is on hand to whisk you up to near the top for sweeping views of Buda and Pest. ⏱ *1 hr. Szent István tér 33.* ☎ *1/317-2859. www.basilica.hu. Free Admission to Basilica, tower Ft 500, Treasury Ft 400. Mon–Fri 9am–5pm, Sat–Sun 10am–4pm. Metro: M1 to Bajcsy-Zsilinszky út. M3 to Arany János utca.*

St. Stephen's Basilica.

The dome in architect Imre Steindl's Paliament.

⑥ ★★★ Parliament. Architect Imre Steindl's mostly neo-Gothic extravaganza dominates Pest's waterfront and bucks the Gothic trend with the 96m/315ft-high dome at its center. While it was once the biggest Parliament in the world when it opened for business in 1896, the building has lost none of its opulence. The exceedingly long corridors of power, the grandiose gold-plated interior and red-carpeted staircases do nothing to instill any form of collective unity between the polarized politicians. While much like any Parliament, should you happen to enter the chamber after a debate, to which the opposition actually shows up, you can almost feel the steam rising as you enter. Look out for the Hungarian crown, a gift from the Pope to King (now Saint) István (Stephen) in the year 1000 to thank him for signing up Hungary to Catholicism. Watch out for protestors outside calling for the current Prime Minister's head. ⏱ *1 hr for tour, 15 min viewing from outside, enquire ahead via internet as Parliament is closed when in session & turn up 10 min before the tour begins. Kossuth tér 1–3.* ☎ *1/ 441-4000. www.mkogy.hu. Tour free for EU citizens, other nationalities Ft 2,640 (students Ft 1,320). Buy tickets at gate X. English tours at 10am,*

Off the Beaten Track

While Budapest is blessed with many outstanding sights, I encourage you to step off the beaten path as and when the mood takes you. Budapest is visually impressive in every direction both deviating from and all along the main route of this particular tour, which features the not-to-be-missed element of the Hungarian capital. The magic of Budapest can also be found in tiny details such as the gargoyles or decorative motifs that adorn the plethora of striking late 18th- and early 20th-century buildings and hidden squares. I have written this guide with that in mind but I suggest you always take a little time to look up and around as you piece together the Budapest jigsaw.

12am, and 2pm daily. Metro: M2 to Kossuth Lajos tér.

7 ★★★ **kids** **Chain Bridge.** This, the pick of Budapest's varied bridges, isn't just an architectural marvel but is the first permanent bridge that linked Buda with Pest, setting in motion their eventual unification. It's also still the best and most scenic way of traversing the Danube to get from Parliament and Pest's old town to the Castle District. The brainchild of István Széchenyi, an anglophile Hungarian Count who sought to bring rural Hungary into the modern age, he employed two designers to build the ornate bridge, each with the name of Clark: William, an Englishman, and Adam, a Scot. The Chain Bridge opened in 1849, during Hungary's War of Independence with Austria and fortunately survived an immediate botched attempt to blow it up, something that the more efficient Germans managed when retreating from occupying the city in 1945. It was soon rebuilt and reopened on its centenary in the original style. Come back at night when it and the Royal Palace are

Funicular in the Castle District.

both lit up dramatically. ⏱ *20 min. Connects Roosevelt tér with Clark Adám tér. Bus 16/105 or Tram 2.*

8 ★★★ **The Castle District.** Bombed, burnt, battered, and rebuilt many times throughout the centuries, the Royal Palace and St. Matthias Church dramatically portray Hungary's trials and tribulations. I suggest you wander the district at your leisure to soak up the history of the place and return later for a more in-depth tour. (See p 60 for a complete tour of this historically rich district.) ⏱ *2 hr. Bus 16 to Dísz tér.*

The Chain Bridge.

The Best **in Two Days**

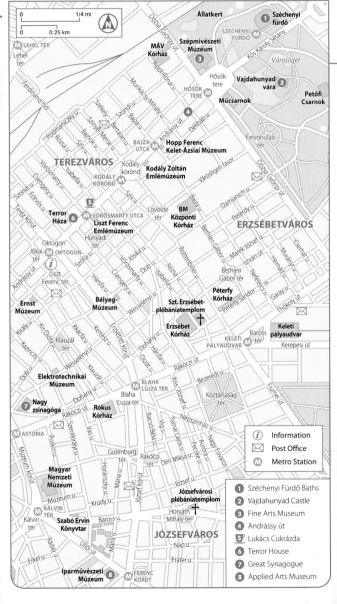

0	1/4 mi
0	0.25 km

Állatkert

① Széchenyi fürdő

SZÉCHENYI FÜRDŐ

Kós Károly sétány

MÁV Kórház

Szépművészeti Múzeum ③

Városliget

Dózsa György út

Lehel tér

Ⓜ LEHEL TÉR

Ferdinánd híd

Podmaniczky u.

Rózsa u.

Szív u.

Székely Bertalan u.

Szondi u.

Bajza u.

Munkácsy Mihály u.

Rippl-Rónai u.

HŐSÖK TERE Ⓜ

Hősök tere

Vajdahunyad vára ②

Petőfi Csarnok

Mücsarnok

Andrássy út ④

Délibáb u.

BAJZA UTCA

Hopp Ferenc Kelet-Ázsiai Múzeum

Felvonulási tér

TEREZVÁROS

Szegfű u.

Bajnok u.

Isabella u.

Kodály körönd

Kodály Zoltán Emlémúzeum

Szív u.

Bajza u.

Városligeti fasor

Dózsa György út

Vörösmarty u.

Csengery u.

KODÁLY KÖRÖND Ⓜ

Damjanich u.

Szondi u.

Eötvös u.

Teréz körút

Terror Háza ⑥

Ⓜ VÖRÖSMARTY UTCA

Liszt Ferenc Emlémúzeum

Lövölde tér

BM Központi Kórház

Bethlen Gábor u.

Peterdy u.

Marek József u.

ERZSÉBETVÁROS

Hunyadi tér

István út.

Cserhát u.

Oktogon

Jókai tér

Ⓜ OKTOGON

ⓘ

Szófia u.

Csengery u.

Vörösmarty u.

Jósika u.

Dob u.

Izabella u.

Porterbieru

Bethlen Gábor tér

Nefelejcs u.

Murányi u.

Hernád u.

Garay u.

Thököly út

Andrássy u.

Liszt Ferenc tér

Hársfa u.

Wesselényi u.

Péterfy Kórház

Péterfy Sándor u.

Ernst Múzeum

Ⓜ

Bélyeg-Múzeum

Szt. Erzsébet-plébániatemplom ✝

Keleti pályaudvar

Király u.

Kós Diósi u.

Akácfa u.

Kertész u.

Erzsébet körút

Dohány u.

Erzsébet Kórház

KELETI PÁLYAUDVAR Ⓜ

Baross tér

Kerepesi út

Klauzál tér

Kazinczy u.

Dob u.

Wesselényi u.

Klauzál u.

Hársfa u.

Rákóczi út

Bezerédj u.

Flumei út

Elektrotechnikai Múzeum

Dohány u.

BLAHA LUJZA TÉR Ⓜ

Blaha Lujza tér

Kiss József u.

Népszínház u.

Köztársaság tér

⑦ Nagy zsinagóga

Rókus Kórház

Rákóczi út

Szentkirályi u.

Vas u.

Barcsó Béla u.

Vig u.

Tolnai Lajos u.

Nagy Fuvaros u.

Aurora u.

Puskin u.

Ⓜ ASTÓRIA

Gutenberg tér

Rákóczi tér

Déri Miksa u.

Teleki u.

József u.

Magyar Nemzeti Múzeum

Horánszky u.

Mária u.

József körút

Józsefvárosi plébániatemplom ✝

Múzeum körút

Krúdy u.

Múzeum u.

Szabó Ervin Könyvtár

Baross u.

Horváth Mihály u.

KÁLVIN TÉR Ⓜ

Kálvin tér

Üllői út

Nap u.

JÓZSEFVÁROS

Erkel u.

Ráday u.

Mária u.

Práter u.

Iparművészeti Múzeum ⑧

FERENC KÖRÚT Ⓜ

ⓘ Information

✉ Post Office

Ⓜ Metro Station

① Széchenyi Fürdő Baths
② Vajdahunyad Castle
③ Fine Arts Museum
④ Andrássy út
5̲ Lukács Cukrázda
⑥ Terror House
⑦ Great Synagogue
⑧ Applied Arts Museum

A fter a hard day of major sightseeing on Day 1, take the plunge and relax in one of Budapest's world-renowned thermal baths, while still admiring its architectural beauty, then get out and about again to uncover some of the unique buildings that reflect the country's varied and troubled past. START: **Take the M1 or 'Millennium Underground' to Széchenyi Fürdő.**

① ★★★ kids Széchenyi Fürdő Baths. The therapeutic waters of this neo-Baroque bathing bonanza will revitalize tired joints and set you up for a fulfilling day. That's providing you don't spend all your time being slow cooked in the hot pools, which will leave you seriously sleepy. Alternate between hot and cold pools, saunas, and steam rooms and take some time out in the medium-temperature pools or just chill out on a deckchair. The most luxurious pool is the outdoor semi-circular one, from which steam dramatically rises in the cold of winter as locals play chess. The whirly pool is great for kids. ⏱ *2 hr. Come early to avoid the crowds, especially in summer.* Állatkerti körút 11. ☎ 1/363-3210. Ft 2,400 with locker, Ft 2,800 with cabin (partial refunds for finishing within

Take a dip in the therapeutic Széchenyi Fürdő Baths.

Vajdahunyad Castle.

2 hr, 3 hr). *6am–10pm daily. Metro: M1 to Széchenyi Fürdő.*

② ★ kids Vajdahunyad Castle. Looking at it now, it's hard to believe that this fairly authentic-looking folly was once made out of cardboard and dates back barely a century. Vajdahunyad Castle went up as a temporary structure as part of the Magyar millennium celebrations in 1896, depicting the various Hungarian architectural styles over the centuries. By 1908, Vajdahunyad had been transformed into a collection of stone replicas representing treasured creations from right across the Magyar realm. Particularly prominent are the ramparts facing the lake from Vajdahunyad Castle and Sighişoara's clocktower, both in present-day

Romania. ⏱ *30 min. Metro: M1 to Hősök tere/Széchenyi Fürdő.*

③ ★★ Fine Arts Museum (Szépmüvészeti Múzeum). The mighty Habsburgs who once ruled as far as Spain and the Netherlands acquired an astonishing collection of impressive art works, many of which found their way here. A tour de force in European art from the 13th to the late 18th centuries, lovers of Madrid's Prado gallery will see similarities with this collection, which is also particularly strong in Spanish masters, with El Greco, Velázquez, Murillo, Ribera, Cano, Zurbarán and Goya all represented. El Greco's *Annunciation*, painted in the late 16th century, is set to heavenly clouds and bright lights (it has a twin in the Prado set to an architectural background), while Velázquez's early work *Peasants Around a Table*, dated around 1619, magically preserves the time-honored tradition of getting stuck into conversation over a few drinks. ⏱ *1½–2 hr. Come early when major temporary exhibitions are running. Dózsa György út 41. Overlooking Heroes Square.* ☎ *1/469-7100. www.szepmuveszeti.hu. Ft 1,200. Tues–Sun 10am–5:30pm. Metro: M1 Hősök tere.*

④ Walk up Andrássy út. You are more than likely to have explored portions of this, the grandest of Budapest's boulevards on Day 1 when checking out the Opera House, but further examination is rewarding. Walking from Heroes Square (p 7, bullet ①) the first stretch is lined with luxurious villas, including Kogart, an arts center and restaurant. Further up, Andrássy út is traversed by Kodály körönd, a striking square of faded but ornately painted town houses. ⏱ *30 min.*

⑤ Lukács Cukrázda. Grab a coffee and a cake or snack at this tastefully restored coffee house that excels in freshly made cakes and pastries and is more laid back than most, being away from the madding crowd at *Andrássy út 70. $.*

⑥ ★★★ Terror House. It's funny how both the Fascists and the Communists both favored this location on classy Andrássy út to do their worst. An address that seems to be cursed, this visually impressive museum caused controversy with its highly politicized opening in 2002. Seen by many as an affront to the re-spun

The cutting edge museum at Terror House.

synagogue not only pioneered a new style of Jewish architecture, it also spawned the father of modern Zionism who was born here, Tivadar Herzl (p 55, bullet ❶). ⏲ *15 min. Dohány utca 2. Metro: M2 to Astoria.*

❽ ★★★ **kids** **Applied Arts Museum.** You might have encountered this remarkable-looking Art Nouveau masterpiece by Ödön Lechner, Budapest's answer to Gaudí, if you took the road in from the airport. Lechner, who also worked on the building's plans with secessionist sidekick Gyula Pártos, created a Hungarian take on the Art Nouveau movement, adding Hungarian folk touches and emphasizing certain eastern influences on Hungary. Accordingly, traces of architectural styles from as far afield as India can be detected, and the bright green and gold Zsolnay tiles that adorn the roof and dome are more Oriental than European. For a tour of the interior go to the dedicated Special Interest Art Nouveau Tour (see p 25, bullet ⓬). ⏲ *1–1½ hr. Üllői út 33–37.* ☎ *1/456-5100. www.imm.hu. Combined ticket, including temporary exhibitions, Ft 2,400. Tues–Sun 10am–6pm. Metro: M3 to Ferenc körút.*

The Great Synagogue.

Hungarian Socialist Party, which once ruled Hungary with an iron fist but has changed beyond recognition, on behalf of their archrivals Fidesz, it was even sponsored by the then Fidesz Prime Minister Victor Orbán. Cynics' claims are backed up by the fleeting coverage of Fascist Hungary and the much denser coverage of the red terror. However, the fascist Hungarian Arrow Cross Party ran the country for only a year, coming into power in 1944, but what a gruesome year that was, with the previously protected Jewish population being shipped off in droves to concentration camps. Politics aside, from the Russian tank that greets you; to the pictures of victims and their jailors; to the industrial and dark classical soundtrack; film footage and interviews; genuine exhibits including Hungarian Nazi Arrow Cross uniforms; and the trip to the cells and gallows, I can't help but feel indignation. ⏲ *1 hr. Andrássy út 60.* ☎ *1/374-2600. www.houseof terror.hu. Ft 1,500. Tues–Fri 10am–6pm, Sat–Sun 10am–7pm. Metro: M1 to Vörösmarty utca.*

❼ ★★ **Great Synagogue.** With its onion domes, Moorish and Byzantine influences, Budapest's great

The impressive entrance to the Applied Arts Museum.

The Best **in Three Days**

Széchenyi lánchíd

József Attila u.

Eötvös tér

József nádor tér

Erzsébet tér

⊠ Dorottya u.

VÖRÖSMARTY TÉR

Vörösmarty tér

Bécsi u.

Apáczai Csere János u.

Pesti alsó rakpart

Vigadó tér

Szervita tér

Régi posta u.

Petőfi tér

Váci u.

Városház u.

Petőfi Sándor u.

Fővárosi Önkormányzat

Gerlóczy u.

DEÁK FERENC TÉR

Deák Ferenc tér

Király u.

Rumbach u.

Holló u.

Dob u.

Károly körút

ⓘ

Nagy zsinagóga

BELVÁROS

ASTORIA

Kossuth Lajos u.

⊠

FERENCIEK TERE

Ferenciek tere

✝ **Ferences templom**

Magyar u.

Belvárosi plébániatemplom ✝

Szabad Sajtó út

Váci u.

Ady Endre Emlékhaz

Duna u.

Egyetemi Könyvtár

Petőfi Irodalmi Múzeum

Márcuis 15. tér

Irányi u.

Buda alsó rakpart

Döbrentei u.

Attila út

Erzsébet híd

Döbrentei tér

Nyáry Pál u.

Váci u.

Molnár u.

Belgrád rakpart

Veres Pálné u.

Szerb templom ✝

Szerb u.

Bástya u.

Király Pál u.

Szt. Gellért Emlékmű

🛥 **Rudas gyógyfürdő**

Havas u.

Só u.

⊠

Vámház körút

GELLÉRTHEGY

Szt. Gellért rakpart

Duna (Danube)

Fővám tér

Vásárcsarnok ❸

Citadella

Csarnok tér

Pesti alsó rakpart

Sziklatemplom ❻

Szt. Gellért tér

Szabadság híd ❹

Kelenhegyi út

Gellért gyógyfürdő ❼

🛥

Szkéne Színház

Mányoki út

Bartók Béla út

Budafoki út

Budafoki út

Műegyetem rakpart

ⓘ	Information
⊠	Post Office
Ⓜ	Metro Station
🛥	Boat Pier

❶	Café Gerbaud
❷	Váci utca
❸	Great Market Hall
❹	Szabadság Bridge
❺	Gellért Hill
❻	Cave Church
❼	Gellért Baths

0 ———— 1/4 mi

0 ———— 0.25 km

N ⊕

After a lot of pacing the streets in Days 1 and 2, here we start with a coffee at one of Budapest's most luxurious coffee houses, followed by a spot of shopping, taking in everything from designer boutiques, folk art shops, and food markets. This tour also gives you the option of ending the day with a swim and a thermal bathe to soothe the joints after scaling the dizzy heights of Gellért Hill. START: **M1 to Vörösmarty tér or Tram 2 to Vigadó tér and walk for two minutes in the opposite direction of the river.**

1 ★ **Café Gerbaud.** Try morning coffee and cake at one of the plushest of the city's illustrious coffee houses. Your biggest decision here will be to work out where to sit to take it all in. This is not the place I would choose to start the day every day—the ornate interior can be a bit over the top—but I find it tasteful enough in small doses to be an ideal treat. Coffee culture is about not only reading papers and devouring Gerbaud's renowned Esterházy and Dobos cakes, but legend has it that young men indicated their availability to well-heeled ladies of pleasure by tipping an excessive amount of sugar into their coffee. In summer, if the wealth of chandeliers, marble tables, fine wood paneling, and stucco ceilings gets a bit much, take to the terrace and sit out on Vörösmarty tér. ⏱ *45 min. Vörösmarty tér 7.* ☎ *1/429-9020. 9am–9pm. Metro: M1 to Vörösmarty tér.*

2 ★★ **kids Váci utca.** Even those who are not shopaholics can easily take in this relatively short shopping street and surrounding area. Starting from Vörösmarty tér, which often has something going on and hosts a Christmas market, you'll find most big international fashion brands from Zara and Mango to Jackpot and H&M. However, most of them offer a somewhat modest selection in comparison to other international cities. Keep an eye out on the side streets for high-end designers. Souvenir shops also abound, though with steep price tags, but if you are into embroidered tablecloths and folk art, then you have come to the right place (see p 77). The shopping street continues on the other side of Szabad-sajtó út, where the vibe is less frenetic. ⏱ *1 hr. Walk through the underpass that connects the two sides of Váci utca. From Vörösmarty tér to Vámház körút. Metro: M1 to Vörösmarty tér (starting point).*

3 ★★ **Great Market Hall.** You may feel like you're walking through an Impressionist painting when the sunlight shines into this beautifully restored king of neighborhood

Café Gerbaud.

Tinned paprika displayed in the Great Market Hall.

catfish crammed in tanks on fish 'death row' downstairs are an uncomfortable sight for some, but hey, at least they're fresh. There are plenty of foodstuffs like paprika, salami, and goose liver to take home, and upstairs look out for folklore and handicrafts hidden among the mountains of tourist goods. There are plenty of nibbles to be eaten upstairs. 🕐 *30 min–1 hr. Vámház körút 1–3.* ☎ *1/366-3300. Mon 6am–5pm, Tues–Fri 6am–6pm, Sat 6am–3pm. Metro: M3 to Kálvin tér. Tram: 2/47/49 to Fövám tér.*

markets. However, it's far from a museum piece; many locals come here to shop for fresh food and it's bustling with life and color. The array of meat on sale shows just how thrifty Hungarians are, as they consider every part of the animal fair game for the pot. The carp and

④ **Walk across Szabadság Bridge.** Buda and Pest are seamlessly connected by this bright green piece of intricate ironwork that joins the Pest's Great Market Hall and its neighbor the Budapest University of Economics (formerly the Karl Marx University) with the Gellért Hotel and the dramatic Gellért Hill of Buda. It was opened by Emperor Franz Joseph in 1896, who actually knocked the last rivet into it. 🕐 *10 min. Starts where Pest's Vámház körút meets the Danube. Tram: 47/49 to Kálvin tér.*

The Gellért Hotel.

5 ★★★ kids **Gellért Hill.** This imposing hill that towers over the Pest waterfront of the Danube has been used to good effect to suppress forces for change. Italian missionary Szent Gellért was reportedly rolled down the hill in 1046 to his death by revolting pagans. The Austrians then built a Citadel from which to lord it over the Magyars *(see p 19)*.

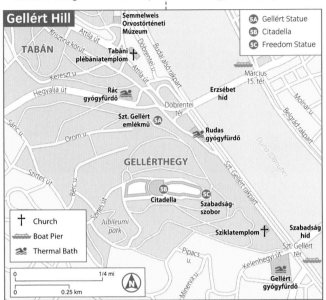

Gellért Hill

TABÁN

Krisztina körút · Attila út

Semmelweis Orvostörténeti Múzeum

Tabáni plébániatemplom †

Kereszt u. · Hegyalja út

Dobrentei út · Buda alsórakpart

Attila út

Rác gyógyfürdő

Márcus 15. tér

Erzsébet híd

Molnár u.

Szt. Gellért emlékmű **5A**

Dobrentei tér

Rudas gyógyfürdő

Belgrád rakpart

Sánc u. · Orom u.

GELLÉRTHEGY

Szirtes út · Berc u.

Citadella **5B**

Szabadság-szobor **5C**

Szt. Gellért rakpart

Duna (Danube)

Szirtes út

Jubileumi park

Sziklatemplom †

Szabadság híd

† Church

Boat Pier

Thermal Bath

Pipacs u. · Minerva u. · Kelenhegyi út

Szt. Gellért tér

Gellért gyógyfürdő

| 0 | 1/4 mi |
| 0 | 0.25 km |

N

5A Gellért Statue
5B Citadella
5C Freedom Statue

To find the Gellért Statue **5A** walk upstream towards the Erzsebet Bridge where you will see the steps leading up. Gellért, who participated in spreading the gospel in 11th-century Hungary on King Stephen's request, met his end being tumbled down the hill (that was subsequently named after him) in a barrel filled with nails—possibly in one of those bum deals whereby your faith supposedly will save you. Ultimately, Christianity won through with Gellért canonized in 1083. The Gellért Statue captures the saint preaching defiantly but precariously on the edge of the hill. It dates back to 1904 and is the work of Hungarian sculptor Gyula Jankovits (1865–1920). Follow the path up and you reach the Citadel **5B** that the Austrians, smarting from the Hungarian Revolution of 1848, built, replete with cannons galore, atop the hill pointing at the Hungarians below. There wasn't much use for it after they patched up their differences in 1867, although German occupying forces utilized it in World War II. The three-level bunker inside the Citadel has waxworks and photos chronicling the Siege of Budapest. Close by and at the peak of the hill, Budapest's very own statue of liberty, the Freedom Statue **5C**, ironically went up in 1947 as a tribute to the Soviet forces that liberated the city from the Nazis. Featuring a woman proffering the palm branch of triumph and not overtly Soviet-looking, it survived the cull of Communist statues from the capital. 🕐 *1–2 hr.*

Relax in style at the Gellért thermal baths.

6 Cave Church. On the way down, just before reaching the Gellért Hotel and Baths, check out this spooky church whose eerie passages dig deep into the hill. Don't be alarmed if a priest appears from nowhere! ⏲ *15 min.*

7 ★★★ Gellért Baths. After another hard day of pounding the streets, the Art Nouveau architecture of the Gellért thermal baths allows you to relax in style but also to see something special. Inside, the central pool is surrounded by Romanesque columns and lions spitting out water, and just for a moment you might expect Elizabeth Taylor's Cleopatra to dive in alongside you. At the end of the pool, the male and female thermal facilities are to the right and left respectively. This is where things start to get really colorful and heated, and I'm not just talking

about the design or decoration, nor the saunas and steam rooms. You can keep your bathing costume on, though many locals like to let it all hang out and dispense with their modesty cloths, although the authorities are said to be cracking down on that sort of thing. The plunge pool is so icy you feel the chill right through your bones, but the thaw of the warm pools is always close at hand. While the waters are supposed to sort out arthritis, blood circulation, and the spine, I say just enjoy them and come out feeling squeaky clean and purified. In summer, be sure to check out the outdoor pools and garden, which is a bit more suited to kids who can enjoy the artificial waves in the main outdoor pool. ⏲ *2 hr. Kelenhegyi út 4.* ☎ *466-6166. Ft 3,100. 6am–7pm. Tram: 47/49/18/19 to Szent Gellért tér.* ●

The Best Art Nouveau

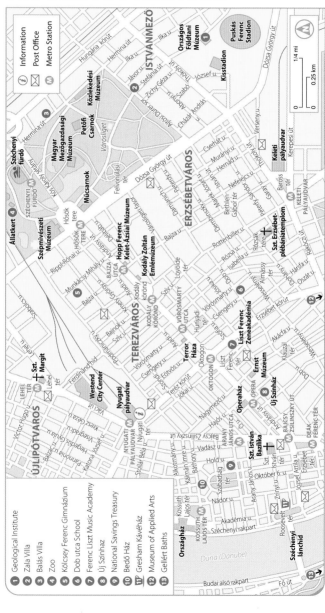

Legend:
- (i) Information
- ☒ Post Office
- Ⓜ Metro Station

1 Geological Institute
2 Zala Villa
3 Balás Villa
4 Zoo
5 Kölcsey Ferenc Gimnázium
6 Dob utca School
7 Ferenc Liszt Music Academy
8 Új Színház
9 National Savings Treasury
10 Bedő Ház
11 Gresham Kávéház
12 Museum of Applied Arts
13 Gellért Baths

Budapest is blessed with many buildings constructed using a unique take on the Art Nouveau movement. Known as szecesszió, it has its own figurehead in Ödön Lechner (1845–1914), Hungary's equivalent to Gaudí. Much of this tour can be managed on foot, which is a great way to see lesser known but still impressive parts of the city you might not normally encounter. START: **M2 to Stadionoak.**

1 kids **★★ Geological Institute (Földtani Intézet).** Ödön Lechner incorporates geological elements such as fossils into his usual folk influences in the eye-catching purple and yellow façade. Should you arrive on a non-visitation day, a look at the entrance hallway will give you an idea of the expressive interior. There's a small Lechner exhibition between floors. ⏱ *30 min. Stefánia út 14.* ☎ *1/251-0999. www.mafi.hu. Ft 250. 10am–4pm Thurs, Sat & Sun. Metro: M2 to Stadionoak.*

2 Zala Villa. A short walk from the Geological Institute, this castle-like structure, noteworthy for the elaborate sculptured motifs of human figures that drape over the wavy arched window, now houses the Libyan Embassy and can be easily viewed from the street. ⏱ *10 min. Stefánia út 111 (corner of Ajtósi Dürer sor).*

3 ★★ Balás Villa. You may have heard of buildings resembling elaborate wedding cakes before, but this Ödön Lechner-designed building, with its various tones of brown, is more of a chocolate cake—and thanks to its angles, a Gothic one at that. It looks out onto the City Park, houses the Braille Institute, and is a short walk from the Zala Villa. ⏱ *10 min. Hermina út 47.*

4 ★ Zoo (Állatkert). Hungarian Art Nouveau often draws on Indian and Oriental elements. Examples of this can be seen at the Zoo's elaborate entrance, which features towers, sculptured elephants, and gruesome gorillas. Like Balás Villa, the Zoo is next to City Park and you can see plenty from the outside. ⏱ *15 min. Állatkerti körút 6. Metro: M1 to Széchenyi fürdő.*

5 ★ Kölcsey Ferenc Gimnázium. After seeing such an ornate zoo, I totally envy Budapest's kids. Just a few minutes' walk away, find the kind of epic and ornate school I'd love to have gone to. However, I'm reliably informed by a Hungarian friend who attended it that it didn't look like this until it was renovated after we both left school in the late 1980s. ⏱ *15 min. Munkácsy Mihály utca 26. www.kolcsey-bp.hu.*

The elaborate entrance to the Zoo.

6 ★★ **Dob utca School.** I'd have no trouble sending my kids to this school. I like the clever and subtle use of brown and blue paintwork that keeps the building subdued enough to be used as a seat of education but still complements the building's wavy and wobbly Art Nouveau aspect. The school's coat of arms, murals of kids playing hide and seek, and marching soldiers provide the perfect finish. *Dob utca 85. www.dobsuli.hu. Tram: 4/6 to Király utca.*

7 **Ferenc Liszt Music Academy.** The parallels with Barcelona and modernismo don't end with Gaudí and Lechner. Aside from the muscular sculptures holding up a seated statue of the man himself, and some handy ironwork, much like Barcelona's famed Palau de la Musica, the real beauty of the Ferenc Liszt Music Academy lies on the inside in its awesome auditorium, which doesn't just look but sounds good too. I suggest you get along to one of the Academy's great value concerts (see Arts & Entertainment p 132) or peek inside during term time. *Liszt Ferenc tér 8. www.lfze.hu. Tram: 4/6 to Király utca.*

8 ★ **Új Szinhaz.** Béla Lajta's compact and somewhat understated

'New Theater' building both fits in and stands out on this narrow side street that runs adjacent to majestic Andrássy. Opened as the Parisiana nightclub in 1909, its charm lies in the domineering sculptured monkeys and the gold and blue organ pipe-like trimmings at the top. *Paulay Ede utca 35. Metro: M1 to Opera.*

9 ★★★ **National Savings Treasury.** Tucked away off the main drag, the front façade is an engaging restrained mix of wavy lines, light colors, Hungarian folk motifs, and Islamic pillars, if such a funky combo can be restrained. Naturally, the bees making honey means money in Lechner-speak. However, the real drama comes with the roof, whereby Lechner deployed the wares of iconic Hungarian ceramics' manufacturer Zsolnay to a more daring end than usual. Here the gentle curves of the façade give way to more stark angles in an eye-catching yellow and green-layered finish. Opened in 1886 as the Royal Hungarian Postal Savings Bank, it now serves as the National Savings Treasury. Although it is closed to the public, you can step in the door for a peek of the interior. 🕐 *15 min. Hold utca 4. Metro: M3 to Arany János utca.*

The Art Nouveau Bedő Ház.

The Museum of Applied Arts.

⑩ ★★ **Bedő Ház.** The Art Nouveau Bedő Ház takes the interactive museum concept a step further. Although the objets d'art are inanimate—Art Nouveau furniture, beds, love chairs, and the like—you can actually sit on or stretch out on them should your desire. The museum stops short of letting you take the exhibits home, but have a word with them and they'll put you in touch with a carpenter who produces replicas. The downstairs café is a good alternative to the pricey Gresham (see p 104). *Honvéd utca 3. ☎ 1/269-4622. www.magyar szecessziohaza.hu. Ft 600. Mon–Sat 10am–5pm. Metro: M2 to Kossuth Lajos tér.*

⑪ **Gresham Kávéház.** This suave coffee house-cum-bistro is housed on the ground floor of the stunningly restored Art Nouveau Four Seasons Gresham Palace hotel (see hotels p 142) and does a noted deluxe burger from sirloin, exquisite sandwiches, and salads. *Roosevelt tér 5–6. ☎ 1/268-5100. $$$.*

⑫ **kids** **Museum of Applied Arts.** I've already introduced you to the exterior of this museum in the Best in Two Days tour (see p 15, bullet ⑧). As you walk through the ornate entrance, sadly the color gives way to a whitewashed interior. In 1920, the wishes of conservative critics were met and the daring design of the interior was painted over. This shouldn't discourage you from entering as, fortunately, they couldn't destroy the essence of the place. The twisty curling shapes, wobbly staircases, and the immense conservatory remain true to their original design. Among the permanent Art Nouveau exhibits look out for the Frigyes Spiegel-designed Art Nouveau Tall Case Clock and lots of groovy defining furniture.

⑬ ★★★ **Gellért Baths.** While much of the Gellért Hotel was bombed to rubble in World War II, the side that houses the baths escaped the worst and remains close to its original Art Nouveau splendor (see p 20, bullet ⑦ and p 27, bullet ①).

The Best Baths

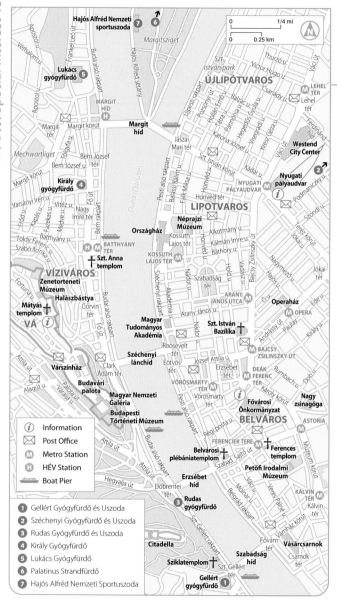

1. Gellért Gyógyfürdő és Uszoda
2. Széchenyi Gyógyfürdő és Uszoda
3. Rudas Gyógyfürdő és Uszoda
4. Király Gyógyfürdő
5. Lukács Gyógyfürdő
6. Palatinus Strandfürdő
7. Hajós Alfréd Nemzeti Sportuszoda

Budapest's thermal baths and lidos have both helped me through many an icy winter and cooled me down in the heat of summer. Each has its own character, while the thermal water itself is prescribed for treating joint problems and arthritis, among other conditions. For a full list of the medical benefits according to each specific water source, go to www.spasbudapest.com. START: **Tram: 18/19/47/49. Bus: 7 to Gellért tér.**

① kids ★★★ Gellért Gyógyfürdő és Uszoda. Although not the best place to come for a good swim, the Gellért offers outstanding single-sex thermal bathing, with the men's side the most lavish. The cold plunge pool is so icy that you can feel your own bones, while the faded grandeur makes the garden a top place to take it seriously easy in the warmer months (p 20, bullet ⑦). *Kelenhegyi út 4.* ☎ *1/ 466-6166. www.gellertbath.com. Admission Ft 2,800 to Ft 3,100 (with cabin rental), Ft 400 refund if you leave within 2 hr. 6am–7pm weekdays; 6am–5pm Sat–Sun (Apr 30– Sept 30). Tram: 18/19/47/49. Bus: 7 to Gellért tér.*

② kids ★★★ Széchenyi Gyógyfürdő és Uszoda. A magnificent neo-Baroque bathing complex,

Neo-baroque bathing at Széchenyi.

but be warned it gets really busy on hot summer days. Go early like the Hungarians do, or consider taking an evening dip. It's at its best in winter with snow on the ground and you're all snug and warm in the outdoor thermal pool (p 13, bullet ①). *Állatkerti körút 11.* ☎ *1/363-3210. www.szechenyibath.com. Admission Ft 2,400 (Ft 2,000 if you leave within 2 hr). Daily 6am–10pm. Some pools and services are only available till 4pm & 6pm & are closed on Sat–Sun. Metro: M1 to Széchenyi Fürdő.*

③ ★★★ Rudas Gyógyfürdő és Uszoda. Plunge into the turquoise water, which is given an extra depth of beauty by the beams of light that penetrate through the holes in the domed ceiling. Surrounded by stone pillars, you can splash back in time. Relax in the main central pool and then dip in and out of the corner pools of varying temperatures. There's a really cold plunge pool around the corner on the way to the changing rooms. A welcome feature of the Rudas is the ward-like lying down room and I heartily recommend a snooze after the extremes your body's just been through. Skip it and you might need an early night. The main bathing chamber features a large central pool and it is also open to women. *Döbrentei tér 9.* ☎ *1/356-1322. Swimming pool 6am–6pm. Steam 6am–8pm. Steam for men Mon, Wed, Thurs, Fri; for women Tues; for both sexes in swimming suits Sat, Sun. Ft 2,200 for the steam (Ft 400 refund if you leave within 2 hr), Ft 1,200 (locker), Ft*

Beams of light penetrate through the ceiling at Rudas Gyógyfürdő és Uszoda.

1,500 (cabin), Ft 1,000 (kids & pensioners) for the swimming pool. Tram: 18/19 to Döbrentei tér. Bus: 5/7/8/86.

❹ ★★ Király Gyógyfürdő.
Under Socialism, the Turkish domed 'King' was a tolerated meeting point for gay men, including certain members of the ruling élite. This carried

on post-1989 and I've heard this place referred to as 'The Queen'. It was so steamy in here that apparently most Budapest heterosexuals have been once, but now, or so I'm told, overtly sexual behavior is no longer tolerated. Smaller than the Rudas, it also takes you back a long way in time. *Fő utca 84.* ☎ *1/202-368. Women Mon, Wed, Fri 7am–6pm. Men 7am–6pm. Men Tues, Thurs, Sat 9am–8pm. Ft 2,300 for over 3 hr; Ft 1,300 within 2 hr. Metro: M2 to Batthyány tér.*

❺ ★ Lukács Gyógyfürdő.
You see many regulars here where it's less touristy and has a mixed bathing option. I like to do a few lengths of one of the rather shortish open-air swimming pools before rewarding myself with the wonders of the interior. You can normally get a lane in the shorter of the two but it is cold, while in the longer pool you'll be competing for space with the leisurely swimmers. There's also a thermal pool with a fun whirlpool for tobogganing with your body. As the whirlpool switches off, people head for the water massage. I love

Lukács Gyógyfürdő.

Enjoy the holiday camp atmosphere at Palatinus Strandfürdő.

lying back, relaxing, as the water surges up to the blurry sound of people's voices. In summer, climb the stairs to the spacious sun terrace that looks out onto leafy Buda. Bikini tops come off here regardless of age, but is by no means obligatory. Inside, the large pool is for taking it easy. Don't stay too long in the hot pool, tempting as it is, beautifully tucked into its own chamber. Brave the steam room, plop straight into the cold plunge pool immediately next to it, and feel purged of all impurities momentarily. It's nice to sit on a bench in the garden and let your pulse return to normal afterwards. *Frankel Leó utca 25–29.* ☎ *1/326-1695. Mon–Fri, Sun 6am–7pm; Sat 6am–5pm. Ft 1,900/1,700 for over 3 hr with cabin/locker; Ft 1,500/1,300 for within 2 hr with cabin/locker. Tram: 4/6 to Margit híd Budai hídfő/18 to Lukács Gyógyfürdő.*

⑥ kids ★★★ Palatinus Strandfürdő. Located on Margaret Island, Palatinus Strandfürdő has a holiday camp atmosphere that you can check into every day in summer. There's a wide range of pools of varying temperatures and a long one for proper swimming, plenty of grass to camp out on, and loads of food stalls and bars. There's even fruit stands. *Margit Sziget.* ☎ *1/340-4505. Go early on very hot days, at weekends, or in school holidays. Daily 9am–7pm May 1–Aug 31. Ft 2,200 with cabin, Ft 1,800 with locker for all day on weekdays; Ft 2,400 with cabin, Ft 2,000 with locker for all day at weekends. Cheaper tickets available for shorter times. Bus: 26 to Palatinus strand.*

⑦ ★ Hajós Alfréd Nemzeti Sportuszoda. Good for a proper swim with its Olympic-sized pool and several others, but also an excellent place to catch some rays. It held the European Swimming Championships in 2006 and has been extended accordingly. The outdoor pools are warm enough for swimming in winter but you can also swim inside. The big pool is sometimes devoted to training but you can usually find somewhere to swim. *Margit Sziget.* ☎ *1/340-4946. Mon–Fri 6am–5pm, Sat–Sun 6am–6pm May–Sep. Mon–Fri 6am–4pm, Sat–Sun 6am–6pm Oct–Apr. Bus: 26 to Hajós Alfréd uszoda.*

Turkish Traces

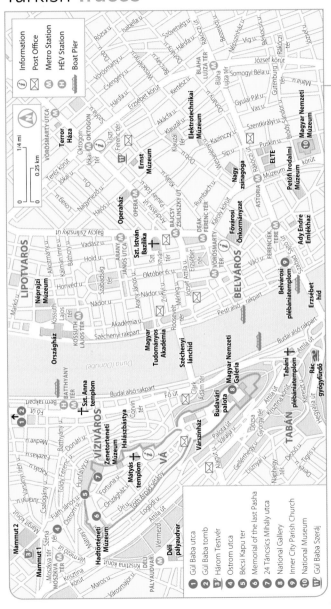

Legend
- (i) Information
- ⊠ Post Office
- ⊙ Metro Station
- ⊙ HEV Station
- ⟷ Boat Pier

N

| 0 | 0.25 km |
| 0 | 1/4 mi |

- ① Gül Baba utca
- ② Gül Baba tomb
- ③ Három Testvér
- ④ Ostrom utca
- ⑤ Bécsi Kapu ter
- ⑥ 24 Táncsics Mihály utca
- ⑦ Memorial of the last Pasha
- ⑧ National Gallery
- ⑨ Inner City Parish Church
- ⑩ National Museum
- ⑪ Gül Baba Szeráj

So often associated with ruling with an iron fist during their 140-year occupation, we start our tour on a street named after Gül Baba, a Turkish fighter, preacher, poet, and influential consort of Suleiman the Magnificent. He even introduced the rose to 'Budin' before falling in the successful invasion of the Castle in 1541. Most of these attractions are located within close proximity to each other.
START: Tram: 4/6 to Margit híd, Budai hidfő.

① ★★ **Gül Baba utca.** I find this a remarkable oasis of tranquility even though it's so close to Margit körút, the noisy Buda thoroughfare. This steep and narrow cobbled Ottomanesque street could be straight out of a hilly Istanbul neighborhood. The preserved wooden bay window at number 30 (unmarked) is directly opposite a very modern but tasteful take on wooden paneling opposite at number 23. ⏲ *15 min. Tram: 4/6 to Margit híd, Budai hidfő.*

② ★ **kids Gül Baba tomb.** Hardly among the most frequented of sights these days, this was once the center of Islamic life in Buda. Gül Baba's pristinely restored mausoleum, which you can enter to take a peek at the colorfully decorated tomb and surrounding grounds, is a rare survivor from a period of history that has been all but wiped from Buda's visage. This Bektashi dervish is credited

with introducing the rose to Buda and the plush surrounding neighborhood is known as Rózsadomb, literally 'Rose Hill'. ⏲ *½ hr. Mecset utca 14/Türbe tér 1.* ☎ *1/326-0062. Ft 500. Tues–Sun 10am–6pm. Bus: 91/191 to Apostol utca. Tram: 4/6 to Margit híd, Budai hidfő.*

③ **kids Három Testvér.** The 'Three Brothers' is a chain of fast food Turkish joints dotted around the city, and this branch fits nicely in with the bustle of the food market above. It has cushions to stretch out on and carpets to add to the color. *Ground floor of Fény utca piac. Lövőház utca 12.* ☎ *1/345-4125. $.*

④ ★ **Walk up Ostrom utca (Siege Street).** Now suitably refueled, I recommend conquering the hill that is 'Siege Street'. You'll be following in the footsteps of the

Statue of Gül Baba.

Have a Bath

On your way down from the Castle District, you can wind down this tour early and take the weight off your feet with a bathe at the once Turkish Rudas baths or Király baths (see entries in Best Baths, p 26). The core of these stunning baths is identical in structure to bathhouses in Turkey, with the exception that the Turks don't bathe in the water as it's considered unhygienic and instead sweat on slabs. These baths have long been converted to pools, but the old atmosphere is retained. Also look out for the disused mushroom-domed former bathhouse opposite the Lukács baths (see p 28, bullet **5**).

Christian international alliance as they headed toward the Vienna Gate where they overpowered the Turks. Look out for Turkish soldier figures carved into the Castle wall. 🕐 *10 min. Metro: M2 to Moszkva tér. Tram: 4/6 to Széna tér/Moszkva tér.*

5 ★★ **Bécsi kapu tér.** Here the Hungarians finally overpowered the Turks to re-enter and reclaim the Castle in 1686. Ironically, after being rebuilt in the years after the liberation of Buda, the gate was taken down in 1896, the year of Hungary's millennium. The particular Vienna Gate (Bécsi kapu) that stands here today dates back to just 1936. As you pass under the gate look for the memorial dedicated to those who fell, not just Hungarians but also other European forces. 🕐 *15 min. Bus: Várbusz 16/16A-116 to Bécsi Kapu ter.*

6 **Memorial of the last Pasha.** It takes a bit of finding but it's there; a Muslim shrine in a typical design within the boundaries of the Castle District, albeit a little tucked away from the busiest parts. Near this spot in 1686, Abdurrahman was defeated and

Memorial of the last Pasha.

killed, bringing 145 years of Turkish rule of Buda to an end. He is apparently held in a certain amount of esteem according to the inscription that refers to him as both a hero and an enemy. 🕐 *10 min. Close to the intersection of Anjou bástya and Országház utca, down the steps from the latter. Bus: 16/16A/116 to Bécsi kapu tér.*

7 **Turkish Head at 24 Táncsics Mihály utca.** Almost blending in with the light-colored stone-work, and right above the Louis XVI doorway of number 24, is the engraved head of an unknown but noble and powerful-looking Turk. Look inside at the remains of the original Gothic sedilla arches, which likely predate the Turkish influence in Budapest. 🕐 *10 min. Bus: 16/16A/116 to Bécsi kapu tér.*

8 ★★ **National Gallery.** I enjoy the dramatic paintings of Magyar battles with the Turks, particularly Benczúr Gyula's enormous canvas *The*

Turkish head at 24 Táncsics Mihály utca.

Recapture of Buda Castle 1686. It makes you think about the history of the spot you are standing on, even if it was painted a couple of centuries later. *(See p 131.)* 🕐 *1 hr. Szent György tér 2 (housed in Royal Palace). Bus: 16/16A-116 to Szentháromság tér.*

⑨ ★★ Inner City Parish Church. Cross the Chain Bridge (p 11, bullet ⑦) and walk downstream, or take Erzsébet hid (bridge to go directly to the Inner City Parish Church. It was the only Christian church fully tolerated by the Turks

Inner Parish Church.

and perhaps has something to do with it being fitted out with a praying niche pointing toward Mecca. You can still see it to the right of the main altar. The surrounding restored Islamic paintwork contrasts sharply with the other more austere half that was destroyed in World War II. 🕐 *15 min. Március 15 tér.* ☎ *1/318-3108. Tram: 2 to Március 15 tér.*

⑩ kids ★★ National Museum. Highlights include the one remaining of a set of three-of-a-kind Turkish leather cloaks in Room 6, the rest of which were lost in a fire at Istanbul's Topkapi Palace. Also of note is the Ottoman art with military arms used by the Turks and the Christian army in Room 8. 🕐 *45 min. Múzeum körút 14–16.* ☎ *1/338-2122. www.hnm.hu. Closed Mon. Metro: M3 to Kálvin tér.*

⑪ ★ Gül Baba Szeráj. You couldn't have a Turkish tour without carpets or at least a chance to have them rolled out temptingly for tea. Unlike Istanbul, they'll only start throwing the carpets down if you're interested in the first place. Serves a selection of plates such as ham, cheese, olives, or hummus and decent wine and beer, too. *Paulay Ede utca 55. No phone. $.*

The Best Coffee Houses

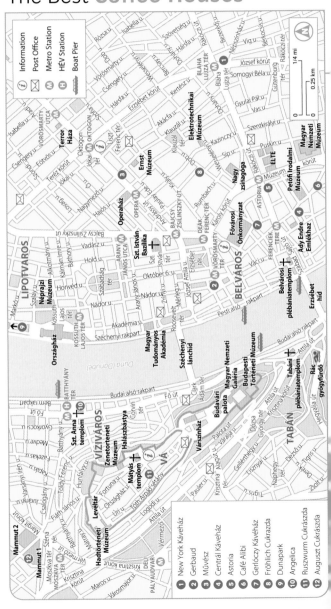

- ⓘ Information
- ☒ Post Office
- Ⓜ Metro Station
- Ⓗ HÉV Station
- ⛴ Boat Pier

- ❶ New York Kávéház
- ❷ Gerbaud
- ❸ Művész
- ❹ Centrál Kávéház
- ❺ Astoria
- ❻ Café Alibi
- ❼ Gerlóczy Kávéház
- ❽ Fröhlich Cukrászda
- ❾ Dunapark
- ❿ Angelica
- ⓫ Ruszwurm Cukrászda
- ⓬ Auguszt Cukrászda

Budapest is legendary for its coffee house (kávéház) culture and for the most part it's an integral part of the locals' lifestyle rather than a cliché to attract tourist dollars. Look out for the cukrászda, basically cake shops, some of which are very cute. I don't suggest following this tour rigidly, rather drop in to one of these coffee houses as and when you're passing.

1 ★★ **New York Kávéház.** The former hangout of cash-strapped writers, poets, and future Hollywood legends back in the fin-de-siècle days. These days, however, fledgling and hard-up film school contemporaries of the likes of Hungarian-born movie mogul Alexander Korda are scared off by the corporate prices. There's no such thing as a preferential writers' menu these days. Before it closed for restoration in the late 1990s it had a real faded grandeur feel, but it's been immaculately restored in its neo-Baroque splendor. Certainly worth a peek but not everyone's cup of tea as it's almost overwhelming with a few too many cherubs for my liking, I prefer something a bit less ethereal. For a real splash in your wallet check out the Deep Water restaurant in the basement. *Erzsébet körút 9–11.* ☎ *1/886-6111. Daily 9am–12pm. Metro: M2 to Blaha Lujza tér.*

2 ★★★ **Gerbaud.** Neo-Baroque bonanza plus some of the best Esterházy and Dobos cakes in town. *(p 17, bullet* **1** *.)*

3 ★ **Művész.** Simple but elegant and old-fashioned in a welcoming way with its arched windows, low-hanging chandeliers, and stripy wallpaper, Művész is just the place to drop into for a coffee and a cake. The action also spills out onto the terrace on classy Andrássy út in summer, although the high ceilings keep it nice and cool inside. Handy for the Opera House. *Andrássy út 29.* ☎ *1/352-1337. Daily 9am–12pm. Metro: M1 to Opera.*

4 ★★★ **Centrál Kávéház.** Another famous institution from Budapest's heyday that was popular with city hacks. The salons of the coffee house are named after the newspaper titles patrons edited and no doubt part worked out of. Central is a bastion of old-world charm and service without overdoing the glitz. Tastefully renovated in 1999, it has high ceilings, arched windows, and all the comfort you need. Centrál is

Coffee and cake at Művész.

Old world charm at Centrál Kávéház.

also great for croissants and has an extensive coffee and wine list. More than a coffee house, it's also a serious dining venue that narrowly missed out on my list of top restaurants. *Károly Mihály utca 9.* ☎ *1/266-2110. www.centralkavehaz.hu. Daily 7am–12pm. Metro: M3 to Ferenciek tere.*

⑤ ★★★ Astoria. Now called the Mirror Café & Restaurant, this place is faded 1920s grandeur personified, with plenty of chandeliers, pillars, and red velvet. It's far from gloomy now they've opened the curtains and with reasonably priced café lattes, it's just the kind of place I like to relax in. Nicely air-conditioned in summer and also quite popular as a restaurant. *Kossuth Lajos utca*

19–21. ☎ *1/889-6002. Daily 7am–11pm. Metro: M2 to Astoria.*

⑥ ★ Café Alibi. A petite modern take on the grand coffee house of old that borrows something of a French bistro feel and is one of my favorites. Located in the quaint University District, Alibi gives you an excuse to take time to chill out. Food is available all day. *Egyetem tér 4.* ☎ *1/317-4209. www.cafealibi.hu. Mon–Sat 8am–9pm, Thurs–Fri 8am–10pm, Sat 9am–9pm, Sun 9am–5pm. Metro: M3 to Kálvin tér.*

⑦ ★★★ Gerlóczy Kávéház. Look out through the high arched windows from this excellent bistro-cum-coffee house onto a charming small square named after the first mayor of Budapest, Károly Kamermayer. The interior is simple and tasteful with a long marble-topped bar and a relaxed Parisian feel. With its free WiFi, many make this their office. In the warmer weather the action spills out right onto the traffic-free square. I also rate this place for a full meal (p 100). *Gerlóczy utca 1.* ☎ *1/501-4000. www.gerloczy.hu. Daily 7am–11pm. Metro: M1/M2/M3 to Deák tér.*

⑧ ★ Fröhlich Cukrászda. The place to come for flavorsome flódni

Relax with a good view of the Danube at Dunapark.

Angelica.

(a triple whammy of apple, poppy seeds, and walnuts, encased in crispy pastry) which is Hungary's contribution to Jewish confectionery. Kosher Fröhlich is nothing plush to look at but has been home baking since 1953 and has a real neighborhood café feel. *Dob utca 22.* ☎ *1/267-2851. Mon–Thurs 9am–8pm, Fri 7:30am–6pm, Sun 10am–4pm. Tram: 4/6 to Király utca.*

⑨ ★ Dunapark. Part modern, part 1930s, Dunapark is housed in a Bauhaus housing block and has plenty of cool Art Deco touches. Big windows provide views to the Danube and the attractive Szent István Park, while the cakes are exquisitely and temptingly presented as you walk in. Less on display is the card room, tucked away upstairs. Increasingly a serious dining establishment. *Pozsonyi utca 38.* ☎ *1/786-1009. www.dunapark kavehaz.hu. Mon–Fri 8am–12pm, Sat 10am–12pm, Sun 10am–10pm. Tram: 2/4/6 to Jászai Mari tér.*

⑩ Angelica. With its view of Batthyány tér and across to Parliament, this is a very special and relaxing place to sit outside in summer. Unfortunately, the eclectic neo-Baroque and 1970s retro décor has been replaced by something much more sterile, although you can

still use your imagination to picture the interior chambers as a one-time crypt. *Batthyány tér 7.* ☎ *1/201-0668. Daily 10am–10pm. Metro: M2 to Batthyány tér.*

⑪ ★★★ Ruszwurm Cukrászda. This bijou and cozy cake joint with low-arched walls dates back to 1827 and retains plenty of old Baroque charm despite its location in the tourist epicenter of Budapest. It looks a bit like a medieval chemist's but, behind the curtain, confectionery from classic recipes by Hungarian cake guru Illés Tóth is being concocted. Cream pastries, Tirol strudels, buttered dough, and many more are presented enticingly above the charming wooden counter—it's easy just to point to the ones you want. For something savory try the scone-like *pogácsa.* *Szentháromság utca 7.* ☎ *1/375-5284. www.ruszwurm.hu. Daily 9am–8pm, closes 7pm off season. 16/16A/116 to Szentháromság tér.*

⑫ ★★ Auguszt Cukrászda. Run by the same family for five generations, this cute confectionery shop now has three branches. It is famous for the E80, a coffee, cream, marzipan, and chocolate cream cake combo. *Fény utca 8.* ☎ *1/316-3817. www.augusztcukraszda.hu. Metro: M2 to Moszkva tér.*

Budapest with Kids

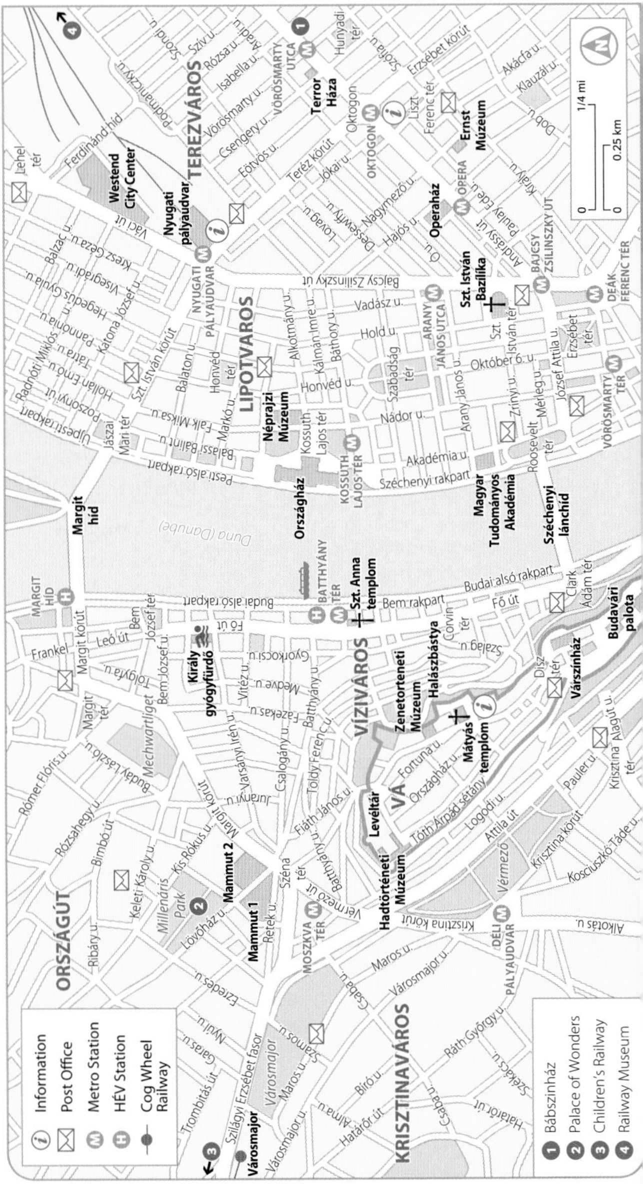
Information
Post Office
Metro Station
HÉV Station
Cog Wheel Railway
1 Bábszinház
2 Palace of Wonders
3 Children's Railway
4 Railway Museum
0 0.25 km
0 1/4 mi
Duna (Danube)
TERÉZVÁROS
LIPÓTVÁROS
VÍZIVÁROS
KRISZTINAVÁROS
ORSZÁGÚT
Margit híd
Széchenyi lánchíd
Országház
Nyugati pályaudvar
Westend City Center
Terror Háza
Ernst Múzeum
Operaház
Szt. István Bazilika
Néprajzi Múzeum
Magyar Tudományos Akadémia
Szt. Anna templom
Király gyógyfürdő
Halászbástya
Zenetorteneti Múzeum
Mátyás templom
Hadtörténeti Múzeum
Levéltár
Várszínház
Budavári palota
Mammut 1
Mammut 2
Millenáris Park
Városmajor

Aside from the green areas of City Park and Margaret Island featured in Best of the Outdoors (p 81), Budapest has a number of other outstanding children's attractions, ranging from good old-fashioned fun to the modern and interactive. START: **M1 to Vörösmarty utca.**

1 ★★ **Bábszí nház (Puppet Theater).** Traditional fairy tales and acclaimed modern adaptations of ballet, opera, and pantomime classics are performed here. Look out for *The Wooden Prince* from local legend Béla Bartók. *Andrássy út 69.* ☎ *1/322-5051. Ft 500–Ft 2,700 depending on the performance. Metro: M1 to Vörösmarty utca.*

2 ★★★ **Palace of Wonders (Csodák Palotája).** Inside, interactive exhibitions keep the children entertained and absorbed, but also teach them scientific principles without them even realizing it. It's part of the Millenáris arts complex, and the outdoors part is great for relaxing with the kids. ⊕ *1 hr. Millenáris, Building D. Fény utca 20–22.* ☎ *1/336-4044. www.millenaris.hu. Ft 1,090, Ft 890. Mon–Sun 10am–5pm, Sat–Sun 10am–6pm. Closed for renewal for two weeks from late Aug. Metro: M2 to Moszkva tér. Tram: 4/6 to Széna tér.*

3 ★ **Children's Railway (Gyermekvasút).** A bizarre but cute hangover from the former system in

Traditional fairy tales at Bábszí nház.

Take a packed lunch aboard the children's train.

which youngsters, or 'pioneers' as they were referred to, were handed the responsibility of running this railway that snakes through the scenic Buda Hills. A packed lunch is a good idea. ⊕ *1 hr. See p 87, bullet* **2**. *Fogaskerekű (Cog Wheel Railway) to Széchenyi hegy.*

4 ★★★ **Railway Museum (Vasúttörténeti Park).** Drive a steam engine, operate a hand wagon, or ride on a horse-pulled tram at Europe's first interactive railway museum, which is home to Hungary's 50-strong operation steam fleet. A vintage diesel shuttle runs to the museum from Nyugati Station 3 Apr–24 Oct. ⊕ *2 hr.* ☎ *06/70-313-4957. Family ticket Ft 1,900. Closed Mon & Dec 19–Mar 14. Interactive rides by appointment only Mar 15–Apr 1 & Nov 2–Dec 18. Apr 3–Oct 24 10am–6pm, otherwise 10am–3am. Bus: 30 to Rokolya utca. Tram: 14 to Rokolya utca.*

The Best Special-Interest Tours

Revolutionary **Budapest**

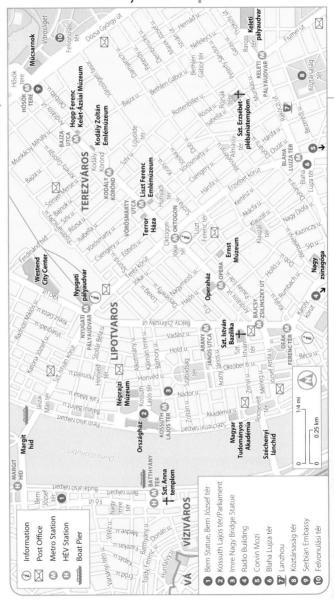

Information
☒ **Post Office**
Ⓜ **Metro Station**
Ⓗ **HEV Station**
⛴ **Boat Pier**

1 Bem Statue, Bem József tér
2 Kossuth Lajos tér/Parliament
3 Imre Nagy Bridge Statue
4 Radio Building
5 Corvin Mozi
7 Blaha Lujza tér
8 Lanzhou
9 Köztársaság tér
9 Serbian Embassy
10 Felvonulási tér

Start at Bem tér (Square), the meeting point of protestors on October 23, 1956 from where the 1956 revolution against the Soviet-backed government and Soviet meddling was initiated. Partially successful demonstrations in Poland, a traditional ally, in June 1956 against Soviet influence made people believe change could come to Hungary. Bem himself was a Polish general who fought with Hungary against Austria in the 1848–9 Revolution. START: **Tram: 4 or 6 to Margit híd, Budai hídfő. Bus: 86 to Bem József tér.**

① **Bem Statue, Bem József tér.** Last time I passed by this legendary square to take a peek at the statue of this swashbuckling Pole, who fought with the Hungarians against the ruling Austrians in 1848, there was just myself and a homeless guy. But don't let that put you off—this is the spot where the spark that triggered the 1956 Revolution was ignited. Rewind to October 23, 1956: in the wake of a promisingly tolerated rebellion in Poland, groups of protestors, starting with students and soon spreading to the masses, met here to stand united against hardcore Communist rule. The Hungarian Revolution was ultimately ill-fated but nevertheless saw many Hungarians escape the tyranny. It also led to a gradual softening of the regime through reforms which saw the implementation of so-called

'goulash Communism'. ⏱ *15 min. Bem tér. Metro: M2 to Batthyány tér. Tram: 4 or 6 to Margit híd, Budai hídfő. Bus: 86 to Bem József tér.*

② ★★★ **Kossuth Lajos tér/Parliament.** After the meeting of minds in front of the Bem Statue in 1956, the crowd that was growing in size and revolutionary fervor marched on to Parliament now demanding change. The bullet holes in the walls of the Agricultural Ministry (p 51, bullet ③) opposite testify to the point where a peaceful demonstration turned violent as Russian tanks and troops fired into the crowd after being shot at from the roof of the Ministry. ⏱ *30 min. Kossuth Lajos tér. Metro: M2 to Kossuth Lajos tér.*

③ **kids Imre Nagy Bridge Statue.** Imre Nagy was Hungary's ill-fated hero of the 1956 Revolution, a

Hungary's ill-fated hero Imre Nagy.

reform-minded Communist Party politician and former leader who sought a new, less strict brand of Socialism for Hungary. He is captured here looking back at Parliament as if thinking about what might have been had the West backed his country in its revolution against Soviet-backed rule. ⏱ *15 min. Vértanúk tere. Corner of Báthory utca, Nádor utca and Vécsey utca. Metro: M2 to Kossuth Lajos tér.*

4 ★★ Radio Building. After things turned nasty at Parliament, the battle was on for control of the airwaves. There may not be many battle scars to see except for a bombed-out wall from the original Radio Building, but I like to wander the streets of this atmospheric neighborhood behind the National Museum and soak up the past. Look out for the beautifully restored palaces either side of the Radio Building's modern entrance. ⏱ *15 min. Bródy Sándor utca 5–7. Metro: M2 to Astoria or M3 to Kálvin tér.*

5 ★ Corvin Mozi. This cinema complex, with its key strategic position next to Pest entry and exit thoroughfare Üllői út, was the site of intense fighting against the Soviets. You won't find any rubble, mortar marks, or bullet holes here, however, as Corvin has been restored to its former glory and function, although you will find a statue of a boy with a rifle that pays tribute to those who fell in the name of the Revolution. ⏱ *15 min. Corvin köz 1. (Close to corner of József körút and Üllői út.)* ☎ *1/459-5050. Metro: M3 to Ferenc körút. Tram: 4/6 to Ferenc korut.*

6 Blaha Lujza tér. After being pulled down with only his boots remaining in place, the Stalin statue was dragged here and smashed up. The square bears the marks of the Communist period. It is also a popular choice for violent protests, but also for partying. The roof of Socialist superstore Corvin is given over to a fabulous expansive rooftop bar in summer. ⏱ *30 min. Blaha Lujza tér. Metro: M2 to Blaha Lujza tér.*

7 Lanzhou. The Chinese poured into Budapest to study and work in the former system. This restaurant may look real simple, but plenty of Chinese are among the patrons and the food is very authentic. A bowl of chicken and noodle soup appears in no time and really tides you over to a bigger meal later. *Luther utca 1/b.* ☎ *1/314-1080. $.*

8 ★ Köztársaság tér. A short walk from Blaha Lujza tér, this is the site where revolutionaries committed brutal executions of the wrong people. At the Communist Party headquarters at number 26 on October 30, 1956 an angry crowd turned on surrendering army officials who they thought were members of the despised secret police. The Socialist Party headquarters was controversially housed here until recently. *Köztársaság tér 26.*

9 ★ Serbian Embassy. Imre Nagy (see bullet **3**), who led Hungary's uprising against the Soviet Union in 1956, sought refuge here at the Yugoslavian Embassy overlooking Heroes Square (p 7, bullet **1**).

Statue of a boy soldier at Corvin Mozi.

Stalin's boots at Blaha Lujza tér.

The country really managed to pursue its own path of market-oriented Socialism, keeping clear of the restraints imposed by the Soviet control organ of the Warsaw Pact. Yugoslav Socialism could have provided an economic and political model something akin to what Imre Nagy, himself a reform-minded Socialist, might have envisaged for Hungary. Thus, the then Yugoslavian Embassy seemed a safe haven for Nagy as the Revolution became a crushed rebellion. Indeed it was safe until he left when he was seized by Soviet agents, and then shipped off to eventual but certain death, despite assurances to the contrary by his successor János Kádár. Often seen as a pawn of Soviet wishes, Kádár is nevertheless credited with reforming the economy along free-market lines, thus making Hungary the so-called happiest barrack in the Communist camp. Opposite at

Heroes Square, in 1989, with the winds of change in the air, Nagy was laid to rest once more with full state honors in front of a huge crowd. Kádár, who relinquished the leadership due to ill health and a struggling economy in 1988, passed away just weeks later on July 6, ironically on the same day as Nagy was acquitted of treason by the Supreme Court. *Dózsa György út 92/b. Metro: M1 to Hősök tere.*

🔟 **Felvonulási tér.** The Hungarian Communist equivalent of Moscow's Red Square is now nothing more than a handy parking spot. However, this is where the annual show parade of Communist might took place, while Party dignitaries watched on from a podium over which a statue of Stalin stood. For a replica of the podium, replete with Stalin's boots, head to Memento Park (p 46, bullet ❶). *Metro: M1 to Hősök tere. Next to Heroes Square.*

Communist Budapest—Behind the Iron Curtain

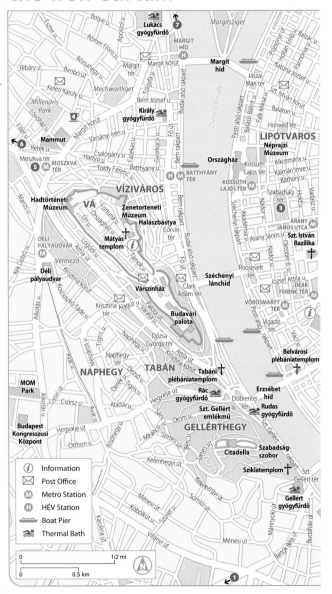

1 Memento Park
2 House of Terror
3 Soviet War Memorial
4 Marxim
5 Moszkva tér
6 Children's Railway
7 Flórián tér
8 PECSA
9 Sporting hero statues

A side from ugly Soviet-era buildings next to fin-de-siècle masterpieces, traces of the past regime are not immediately apparent so this tour requires a bit of traveling. Most of the Communist statues were dragged off to Memento Park on the outskirts of Budapest, which is where we start our tour. START: **Bus: 150 from Kosztolányi Dezső tér to Memento Park.**

① ★★★ Memento Park (includes Statue Park).

Hungarians are reflective about their history. Instead of destroying all traces of the past, the despised statues of the former regime were dragged here to stare at each other. You're greeted by an imposing statue of Lenin and a funky Cubist one of the Communist Manifesto authors Marx and Engels as you enter the Park. My favorite has to be the Herculean worker figure of the Republic of Councils Monument (statue no. 33) in full flight, sprinting for the Communist cause. The statues still get the emotions going and it's easy to get indignant at the statue commemorating Soviet/Hungarian cooperation whereby a worker shakes hands with a beefy Soviet soldier (statue no. 4), almost visually suggesting don't mess with me and you'll be fine. I especially like the

Statue at Memento Park.

Park toward sunset, when you can best feel their menace and collective might bearing down on you. ⏱ *1 hr. Corner of Balatoni út and Szabadkai utca.* ☎ *1/424-7500. www.mementopark.hu. Ft 1,500. Daily 10am–dusk. Bus: 150 from Kosztolányi Dezső tér to Memento Park (25 min). Dedicated bus: Ft 3,950 including return trip via direct bus from Deák tér (bus departs 11am all year, plus 3pm in July & Aug).*

② ★★★ House of Terror.
A cutting-edge museum detailing the horrors of oppressive regimes that occurred on this site. *See p 14, bullet* ⑥.

The Soviet War Memorial.

Óbuda—Traces of 'Old Buda' Behind the Socialist Façade

Communist town planners really took to consigning Óbuda's one-time beauty to the history books; however, nearby pockets of charm thankfully remain. Baroque Fő tér has survived intact and still looks striking despite the ugliness of huge tower blocks bearing down on it. In addition to cute old houses, Roman ruins are also spattered around the 'prefab paradise'. The Amphitheater off Pacsirtamező (Intersection of Viador utca) is said to have been as big as the Coliseum, while the densest collection of Roman ruins can be found at Acquincum. Hercules Villa (Meggyfa utca 21) was closed due to 'technical problems' at the time of writing, but the impressive mythological floor mosaics could be viewed with a minimum group of six by calling ☎ 1/430 1-1081. The museum itself is very retro and blends in well with the Socialist-era housing blocks of the area.

❸ ★ Soviet War Memorial.

This war memorial is a notable survivor of the purge of the Socialist-era statues that found their way to Memento Park. Controversial, thanks to the Soviet 'liberators' who overstayed their welcome by more than 40 years, the memorial still stands proud, although unsurprisingly there is a movement underway to tear it down. The wounds of Soviet influence are still raw and it was severely vandalized during the anti-government riots of 2006 and is now ring-fenced. Interestingly, the final touches to its refurbishment were applied when Socialist Prime Minister Ferenc Gyurcsány was in Moscow. The memorial is directly opposite the US Embassy, where Cardinal Mindszenty sought refuge in 1956 as the Soviets extinguished the fire of the uprising. He stayed for 15 years in a big finger-up to the suppression of the church. ⏱ 10 min. Szabadság tér. No phone. Metro: M2 to Kossuth Lajos tér or M3 to Bajcsy-Zsilinsky út.

❹ ★★ Marxim.

Communist-themed pizzeria and pub with barbed wire and chicken wire separating the booths, decked out with plenty of Socialist-period memorabilia. The pizza is chunky American rather than Soviet. Feel free to write your messages on the walls. *Kis Rókus utca 23.* ☎ 1/316-0231. $.

Communist-themed bar Marxim.

Moszkva Tér.

5 Moszkva tér. Moszkva tér is a charming old square surrounded by dramatic buildings, such as the castle-like Post Office admin building. The masterpiece of the square, however, is the surge of Socialist-Realism that emerges from the middle square in the form of the space age underground station. 'Moscow Square' is a busy and bustling meeting point and transport hub—the kind of place where people come to sign up for a day's illegal work—and therefore is subject to regular police raids. The escalator to the underground descends from such a height it can make you dizzy. ⏱ *15 min. Moszkva tér. Metro: M2 to Moszkva tér.*

6 ★★ Children's Railway. A cute hangover of the previous political system, the Children's Railway was run by the Communist 'pioneer' youth movement that delivered organizational skills and an understanding of responsibility to future Party members (p 87, bullet ②). ⏱ *1 hr. Fogaskerekű (Cog Wheel Railway) to Széchenyi hegy.*

7 ★★ Prefab housing overlooking Flórián tér, Óbuda. A bizarre sight that bears the architectural stamp of two contrasting empires: Roman and Soviet. The prefab housing block is among the city's drabbest and is supposedly Eastern Europe's longest connected estate—but no one is shouting this from the rooftop. It's a far cry from what's left of the classical columns that make up the ruins of a Roman settlement in the square it overlooks. Tucked under the flyover you'll find the remains of Roman baths. ⏱ *30 min. HÉV to Árpád híd.*

8 ★ PECSA. This Socialist-era music venue replete with a funky exterior is still going strong and you can see some big names here, both on the indoor and outdoor stage. On weekend mornings it's the place to buy Socialist bric-à-brac (see Best Shopping p 65). *Zichy Mihály utca.* ☎ *1/363-3730. Metro: M1 to Széchenyi fürdő. Map p 70.*

9 ★★ kids Sporting hero statues. I've always found these statues of Socialist sporting titans inspiring. They almost seem to transcend political ideology, although sport was used to express supposed superiority of the political left. Nevertheless, they stand as tributes to an impressive sporting past. Now used as a backdrop for concerts and events, you can normally get in to see them. The statues are part of the Ferenc Puskás stadium, which has many interesting Socialist design elements. ⏱ *30 min. Ifjúság út 1–3. 100m on right from entrance. Free Admission. Metro: M2 to Stadionak.* ●

3 The Best
Neighborhood Walks

Belváros

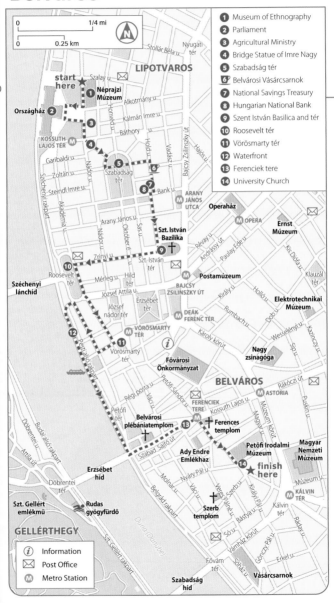

1 Museum of Ethnography
2 Parliament
3 Agricultural Ministry
4 Bridge Statue of Imre Nagy
5 Szabadság tér
6 Belvárosi Vásárcsarnok
7 National Savings Treasury
8 Hungarian National Bank
9 Szent István Basilica and tér
10 Roosevelt tér
11 Vörösmarty tér
12 Waterfront
13 Ferenciek tere
14 University Church

You won't be able to miss the size and extravagance of Hungary's neo-Gothic Parliament that looks built for a superpower—which in fact Hungary was when it was completed in 1904. However, this is just the start of epic central Pest and on this tour you'll see other landmark buildings from Budapest's heyday. Despite the distinct air of faded grandeur, much of this neighborhood's history lies nearer to the present. START: **Metro: M2 to Kossuth Lajos tér/Tram: 2 to Szalay utca.**

❶ Museum of Ethnography. This impressive neo-classical building helps counterbalance the power of the Parliament opposite and is situated in yet another beautiful Budapest square. On the inside, its permanent exhibitions help give a perspective on the maverick Magyars. ⏱ *15 min–1 hr (depending on whether you visit the exhibition). Kossuth Lajos tér 12. www.neprajz. hu. Admission Ft 800. 10am–6pm. Closed Mon. Metro: M2 to Kossuth Lajos tér/Tram: 2 to Szalay utca.*

❷ ★★★ Parliament. Sprawling in size and style, Hungary's giant Parliament building signifies Hungary's pre-Trianon might. The Trianon Treaty of 1920 might have seen Hungary lose two-thirds of its

Imre Nagy looks over to the parliament building.

territory and around the same in population, but the Parliament is still there to be savored in all its glory. See p 10, bullet ❻.

❸ kids Agricultural Ministry. I always make a beeline for the arches of the Agricultural Ministry and walk along the covered passage watched by the busts of notable Magyar agriculturalists. Look out for the marked bullet holes from the 1956 uprising-cum-revolution against the Soviets. *Kossuth Lajos tér 11.*

❹ kids Bridge Statue of Imre Nagy. Hungary's ill-fated leader is captured here in a moving forlorn pose (p 41, bullet ❸). *Vértanúk tere. Corner of Báthory utca, Nádor utca & Vécsey utca.*

❺ ★ kids Szabadság tér. I like to grab a coffee at Café Farger at Zoltán utca 18, sit outside and contemplate this grand and spacious square's contradictions. The controversial Soviet War Memorial pays thanks to the Soviet forces for liberating Hungary from the Nazis, though ironically they then effectively stayed for more than 40 years. The memorial faces the old Cold War foe in the form of the American Embassy, which was severely vandalized in the 2006 riots for its association with the Socialist-led government. The then Prime Minister, Ferenc Gyurcsány, was caught on tape at a supposed closed party convention admitting that his government had screwed it up and done nothing for the country. In

Bees making honey on the façade of the National Savings Treasury.

tandem, in perhaps the most drastic action of the 2006 anti-government insurrection, the building that houses the Hungarian State Television (MTV) was stormed by right-wing protestors and curious members of the onlooking crowd. The vast structure was built by Ignác Alpár, also of National Bank fame, and once housed the stock exchange. *Szabadság tér*.

6 **Belvárosi Vásárcsarnok.** Head to the far end of this inner-city food market for a Hungarian version of fish 'n' chips, next to which there's a hole-in-the-wall eatery serving hearty Hungarian classics. Also, stalls selling deep-fried dough (lángos), sausages galore, and cheap Chinese. *Hold utca.* ☎ 1/332-3976. 6:30am–5pm Mon, 6:30am–6pm Tues–Fri, 6:30am–2pm Sat. Closed Sun.

7 ★★★ **National Savings Treasury.** The depictions of bees making honey, symbolizing moneymaking, can be seen on the exterior walls of this Art Nouveau masterpiece from Ödön Lechner, Hungary's answer to Gaudí. (See p 15, bullet **8**.)

8 **Hungarian National Bank.** Like the epic Parliament building, the stature of Hungary's Central Bank is reflected in the size and drama of the building. The building was originally constructed as the headquarters for the Budapest network of the Austro-Hungarian Bank in 1905. An eclectic and empowering palatial structure, it was designed by the financial institution architect supremo Ignác Alpár and stands in contrast to the slick, modern Bank Center, opposite it, that went up some 90 years later. *Szabadság tér 8–9*.

9 ★★★ **Szent István Basilica and tér.** My first memory of Saint Stephen's Basilica (p 9, bullet **5**) is from the early 1990s when it was a neglected, blackened structure—a far cry from its gleaming condition now. The square itself is also looking good these days and appears to have been hand-polished. *Szent István tér*.

10 ★★ **Roosevelt tér.** Comprising the opulent Academy of Sciences, on the left-hand side as you face Pest from the number 2 tram stop, and the stunningly restored Art Nouveau Four Seasons Gresham

Palace hotel opposite, the new office building between them has enhanced the square no end. The southern side, however, is the realm of the big hotels built to Socialist-Realist specifications. *Roosevelt tér.*

⑪ ★ **Vörösmarty tér.** One of the many mini-centers of Pest that is looking considerably better and more like an old town square now that a tasteful modern structure (parallel with the Danube, on the side closest to the river) has replaced the former Socialist-era monstrosity. Toward Christmas an ever-improving Christmas market pops up on the square where shoppers keep the cold off by imbibing mulled wine (forralt bor). *Vörösmarty tér.*

⑫ ★ kids **Walk the waterfront.** Pretty Vigadó tér is named after the arch-windowed and pillared concert hall.

⑬ ★★★ **Ferenciek tere.** This square is notable for Pest's very own twin towers, the ornate Habsburg-period, neo-Renaissance Klondit and Matilda. They lie directly opposite each other, either side of the busy Szabadsajtó út, and form

Szent István Basilica.

an impressive exit gate from Pest over Erzsébet Bridge. The view looking between the buildings to the more modern bridge and to Gellért Hill is striking. Párizsi udvar (at Ferenciek tere 10–11/Petőfi Sándor utca 2–8) is a grandiose forerunner of the modern shopping mall, and seems to be lifted straight from turn-of-the-century Paris. It was built on the eve of World War I during the last phase of Budapest's epic Austro-Hungarian construction frenzy. This under-utilized shopping arcade is finished in polished dark colors that resemble the interior of a cathedral and is topped off by intricate and sumptuously colored glasswork.

⑭ ★★ **University Church.** A Baroque beauty tucked away in this less frequented but atmospheric corner of District V. Famous Hungarian saints and mythical Magyars feature in the side chapels while fading Baroque brushwork makes this the kind of church I like. Ask the friendly gentleman—who is eager to try out his English—if you can see the cloister. ⏱ *15 min. Free admission.* *Egyetem ter.*

Locals rest on the steps at Vörösmarty tér.

The Jewish **Quarter**

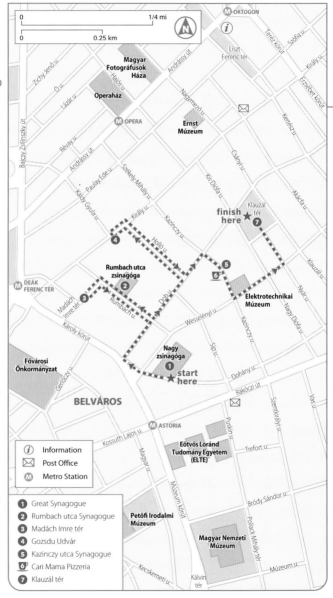

Budapest is home to Central and Eastern Europe's largest Jewish community and this neighborhood in District VII is its core. While you're more than likely to visit one of its hip nightspots, it is well worth looking and nibbling around in the daytime when it's steeped in atmosphere. Magnificent synagogues surrounded by crumbling buildings are the norm and it's not hard to imagine that this was once a ghetto. START: **M2 to Astoria then walk a couple of minutes to the Great Synagogue at Dohány utca 2 on the corner of Wesselényi utca.**

❶ ★★★ Great Synagogue.

Somewhat tucked away off the main drag, the Great Synagogue has been beautifully restored and reopened in 1995. It also houses the Hungarian Jewish Museum. For me the real drama of the building, which is the world's second largest synagogue after New York's, is in the Moorish and Byzantine exterior. Some Gothic touches, like the arched windows and trefoil ledge, are also apparent, although the interior is suitably lavish. The twin onion-domed towers crown the building's oldest part, designed by Viennese Ludwig Förster, while the wing that houses the museum to the left side was added in 1931. After its consecration in 1859, the revolutionary form influenced synagogue design internationally. However, it's not just the architecture of this Neolog house of worship that changed the course of history: Tivadar Herzl, the father of modern Zionism, who sought the establishment of a Jewish country in the Middle East, was born within its grounds in 1860. A central part of the ghetto in World War II, the back courtyard has a cemetery where a couple of thousand Jews, who perished in atrocious conditions, are buried. The leaves of Imre Varga's moving metallic weeping willow contain names of those who died in the holocaust. 🕐 *1 hr. Go early at 10am on weekdays before crowds in summer. Dohány utca 2 (corner of*

The Great Synagogue and Hungarian Jewish Museum.

The stunning tunnel-like courtyard Gozsdu Udvar.

Wesselényi utca). Admission Ft 1,600. Metro: M2 to Astoria.

2 Rumbach utca Synagogue. A symbol of compromise between squabbling factions of the local Jewish community, Viennese Otto Wagner built the so-called 'status quo' synagogue in 1872 using bright Moorish colors and topping the structure with a pair of classic mosque-like towers. Although it no longer functions as a synagogue, visitors are sometimes allowed in to

Rambach utca Synagogue can sometimes be entered for a small fee.

view the colorful turquoise-dominated interior for a small fee. *Rumbach utca.*

3 Arch between buildings at Madách Imre tér. The huge archway that connects the towering bright red-brick townhouses that look out onto the central boulevard of Károly körút was to have been the entry point to a new grand boulevard that would have graced Jewish Budapest. However, the tragic events of World War II put paid to that idea. The view back through the archway to Gellért Hill is spectacular, but the boulevard peters out quickly when a modern banking center crosses its path. *Madách Imre tér.*

4 ★★★ Gozsdu Udvar. Continue down Rumbach utca and walk up Király utca to number 13. This stunning tunnel-like courtyard network, which has been used in numerous films, connects the upcoming and trendy Király utca with the still ghetto-like Dob utca. Now it's gone a bit upmarket (the idea is to turn it into a shopping arcade) compared to its state of decayed beauty of just a few years back, when it was home to just one solitary obstinate tenant who resisted the developers. The developers

Best of the Rest of Jewish Budapest

The functioning synagogue at Frankel Leó út 49 is a bizarre sight. Passing many times from the Danube side, onto which the back juts between two large townhouses, I thought it was simply bricked up. However, from the Frankel Leó side there's a fully functioning synagogue amazingly tucked inside a courtyard. The main Budapest Jewish cemetery at Kozma utca 3 in District X (☎ 1/262-4687) contains some stunning Art Nouveau tombs, especially that of the Schmidl family, which is the work of Hungary's secessionist Kings Lechner and Lajta who used Zsolnay ceramics in the design. The Holocaust Memorial Center at Páva utca 39 in District IX (☎ 1/455-3333) charts the tragic path from deprivation of rights to genocide for local Jews and Roma. Another chilling reminder of many of the local Jewish population's terrible fate comes from the permanent 'Shoes on the Danube Promenade' memorial, a few hundred yards from Parliament in the direction of the Chain Bridge. This 40m/130ft row of sculpted iron shoes, created in 2005 by Gyula Pauer and Can Togay, stands as a memorial to victims of Hungary's Nazi party, the Arrow Cross, who in 1944 and 1945 shot Jews after making them take off their shoes. They then fell straight into the river.

got their way, of course, but, fortunately, much of the old atmosphere remains. So far only one bar, Konczi Kert, near the Király utca entrance, is open (summer 2008). *Enter from Király utca 13 or Dob utca 16. www.gozsduudvar.hu.*

⑤ Kazinczy utca Synagogue. I just love how the Art Nouveau movement influenced the design of the city's synagogues. The Kazinczy Synagogue boasts an awesome Art Nouveau façade, half hidden down this narrow street, which is all the more remarkable when you think that this was commissioned by orthodox traditionalists. ⏱ *30 min. Kazinczy utca 29–31.10am–3:30pm Mon–Thurs, 10am–12:30pm Fri & Sun. Admission Ft 800.*

⑥ ★★ Cari Mama Pizzeria. Quick and crispy Kosher pizza, sandwiches, salads, fried eggs, and

pastries, although the latter tend to have sold out by midday. The smoked salmon 'Smokey' pizza is my, and many other people's, favorite. *Kazinczy utca 28.* ☎ *1/342-0231. $.*

⑦ kids Klauzál tér. This big, ambient square has seen a lot in its history. The ironwork doorway into the indoor market hall retains some pre-war charm, although there's a lack of market stalls with the space mainly taken up by a supermarket. For atmosphere head a few doors down to the Kádár Étkezde (p 100) for a late lunch (closes 4:30pm). Forget retro, this is the genuine article with pictures of past celebrities, soda siphons to dilute raspberry cordial (málna szörp), and patchwork tablecloths. You still pay the man on the door on the way out for what you've had. *Klauzál tér.*

The **Watertown (Víziváros)**

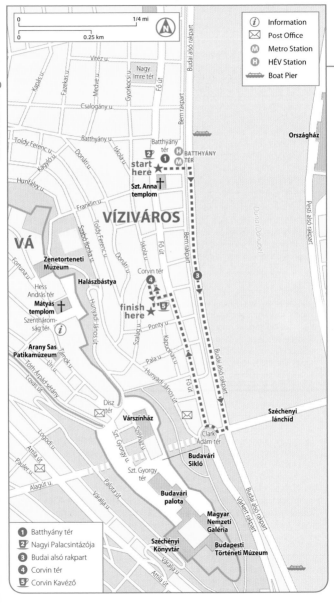

(i)	Information
⊠	Post Office
Ⓜ	Metro Station
Ⓗ	HÉV Station
🚢	Boat Pier

0 — 1/4 mi
0 — 0.25 km

Vitéz u.
Kapás u.
Fazekas u.
Medve u.
Gyorkocsi u.
Nagy Imre tér
Fő út
Csalogány u.
Batthyány u.
Batthyány tér
Toldy Ferenc u.
Donáti u.
Iskola u.
BATTHYÁNY TÉR
Kagyló u.
Hunfalvy u.
Franklin u.
Szt. Anna templom
VÍZIVÁROS
VÁ
Zenetörteneti Múzeum
Szabó Ilonka u.
Toldy Ferenc u.
Donáti u.
Iskola u.
Fő út
Bem rakpart
Budai alsó rakpart
Halászbástya
Corvin tér
Hess András tér
Mátyás templom
Szentháromság tér (i)
Hunyadi János út
finish here ★
Ponty u.
Arany Sas Patikamúzeum
Tárnok u.
Úri u.
Tóth Árpád sétány
Lovas út
Szalag u.
Kapucinus u.
Pala u.
Hunyadi János út
Fő út
Dísz tér ⊠
Várszínház
Logodi u.
Szt. György u.
Színház u.
⊠
Attila út
Pauler u.
Szt. György tér
Szt. György u.
Budavári Siklo
Alagút u.
Palota út
Budavári palota
Váralja u.
Magyar Nemzeti Galéria
Széchényi Könyvtár
Budapesti Történeti Múzeum
Váralja u.
Attila út

Budai alsó rakpart
Bem rakpart
Országház
Pesti alsó rakpart
Duna (Danube)
Budai alsó rakpart
Széchenyi lánchíd
Clark Ádám tér
Várkert rakpart

start here ★

➊	Batthyány tér
➋	Nagyi Palacsintázója
➌	Budai alsó rakpart
➍	Corvin tér
➎	Corvin Kavézó

I love wandering this gem-packed small area wedged between the Castle District and the Danube, especially at the weekend when all's peaceful. The main sights are down toward the river but I also recommend climbing the steep picturesque streets, particularly Ponty utca (Carp Street) that starts down on Fő utca. START: **M2 to Batthyány tér.**

1 ★★★ Batthyány tér. Strikingly situated directly opposite Parliament (see p 10, bullet **6**), which effectively makes up the fourth corner of the square despite being on the other side of the Danube, Batthyány tér is a haven of Baroque beauty in this busy part of Buda. The Baroque attractions include St. Anne's church and a number of colorful houses, including one sunk below street level. Sip a coffee in the famous Café Angelica (p 37, bullet **10**) and you'll be sitting in the church's former crypt. The impressive market hall is a more recent addition. *Batthyány tér.*

2 Nagyi Palacsintázója. Fast food Hungarian style with sweet and savory pancakes, plus salads and filled jacket potatoes. *Batthyány tér 5. $.*

3 Budai alsó rakpart and the Chain Bridge. Stroll along next to the tree-lined tramline overlooking the Danube to the Chain Bridge. Budapest's most famous bridge features two arched neo-classical buttresses that rise high above the water. Often compared to a pair of imperious 'silent' lions, they were sculpted by János Marschalkó who curiously didn't give them tongues. There's also plenty of both solid and intricate ironwork hanging from the buttresses. See p 11, bullet **7**.

4 ★ Corvin tér. Here you'll find another haven of Baroque buildings clustered either side of the square, as well as the eclectic-looking turn-of-the-century Budai Vigadó at number 8, which is home to the Hungarian National Folk Ensemble. It's worth peeking inside for the Art Nouveau interior decoration, and grand staircases. I find the square at its best on weekends when the traffic is sparse.

5 Corvin Kávézö. Bijou café right on pretty Corvin tér that enables you to refuel while admiring the Baroque houses or the view up to Castle Hill. *$.*

The bustling Batthyány tér.

Batthyány tér

The Castle **District**

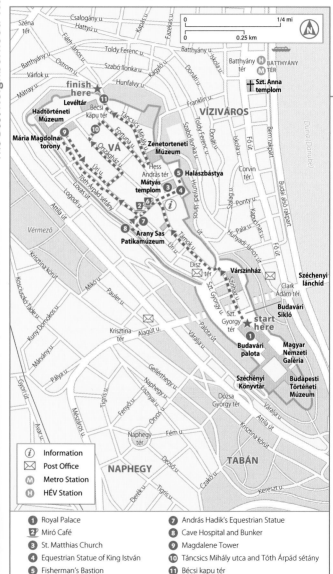

0 1/4 mi
0 0.25 km

Széna tér
Csalogány u.
Hattyú u.
Fiáth János u.
Toldy Ferenc u.
Batthyány H BATTHYÁNY
tér M TÉR
Ostrom u.
Batthyány u.
Szabó Ilonka u.
Kagyló u.
Donáti u.
Batthyány u. Iskola u.
† Szt. Anna
templom
Várfok u.
Várfok u.
Mátray u.
Hunfalvy u.
finish here
Franklin u.
Iskola u.
Fő út
Szabó Ilonka u.
VÍZIVÁROS
Toldy Ferenc u.
Buda alsó rakpart
Duna (Danube)
Levéltár
Bécsi kapu tér
Táncsics Mihály u.
Hadtörténeti Múzeum
Fortuna u.
Zenetorteneti Múzeum
Corvin tér.
Bem rakpart
Mária Magdolna torony
VÁ
Országház u.
Hess András tér
Mátyás templom
5 Halászbástya
n. terez
Úri u.
Tóth Árpád sétány
Lovas út
Hunyadi János u.
Ponty u.
Kapuchres u.
Buda alsó rakpart
Lopodi u.
Attila út
Vérmező
8 Arany Sas Patikamúzeum
Fernok u.
Úri u.
Pala u.
Pala u.
Hunyadi János u.
Fő út
Krisztina körút
Mikó u.
Dísz tér
Szt. György u.
Várszínház
Széchenyi lánchíd
Kosciuszko Táde u.
Pauler u.
Szinház u.
Clark Ádám tér
Kuny Domokos u.
Krisztina tér
Alagút u.
Szt. György u.
Váralja út
Palota út
Budavári Sikló
Márvány u.
Pálya u.
Gellérhegy u.
Szt. György tér
start here
Budavári palota
Magyar Nemzeti Galéria
Győri út
Avar u.
Tigris u.
Naphegy u.
Lisznyai u.
Orvos u.
Fém u.
Dózsa György tér
Váralja u.
Attila u.
Krisztina körút
Széchényi Könyvtár
Budapesti Történeti Múzeum
Fenyő u.
Mészáros u.
Naphegy tér
NAPHEGY
Dezső u.
TABÁN
Derék u.
Tigris u.
Czakó u.
Kereszt u.

(i) Information
⊠ Post Office
Ⓜ Metro Station
Ⓗ HÉV Station

1 Royal Palace
2 Miró Café
3 St. Matthias Church
4 Equestrian Statue of King István
5 Fisherman's Bastion
6 Ruszwurm Cukrászda
7 András Hadik's Equestrian Statue
8 Cave Hospital and Bunker
9 Magdalene Tower
10 Táncsics Mihály utca and Tóth Árpád sétány
11 Bécsi kapu tér

The opulence of the repeatedly razed and rebuilt Royal Palace and St. Matthias Church dramatically portrays Hungary's trials and tribulations. They are, however, just the beginning of this historic and richly bequeathed district. Being Budapest's most tourist-infested area I recommend an early start, but it's also great at night. START: **Bus 16/16A/116 to Dísz tér. There is also the Sikló (funicular) for Ft 800 to the Castle gate from Clark Ádám tér below the Castle, which is quite a bit more expensive than the bus.**

① ★★★ **Royal Palace.** The imposing and multi-faceted Royal Palace may have become a Royal Residence in the 14th century but it dates back further to the 13th-century Mongol invasion of Hungary. The Palace took a serious battering when the Turks were evicted in 1686, and the first attempts at rebuilding it were much more austere than the opulence you see today. Its grand design was literally made fit for a King—Austria's Franz Josef I—by leading local architects after the Austro-Hungarian Compromise of 1867. If you alight from the funicular right next to the entrance you're greeted by a statue of the mythical Magyar bird the Turul, which looks like it's about to fly away from all the tourists. The sweeping views down the Danube and over to Pest from the Castle Gardens, which you enter through an ornamental gate, help put much of the Budapest jigsaw into place. The main attraction on the inside of the Royal Palace is the National Gallery (p 131). In the outer courtyard, Alajos Stróbl's King Matthias's Fountain dates back to 1904 and fits perfectly in the niche in the Palace wall. The ramparts are much older, and the stretch south of Szent György tér dates back to Sigismund of Luxembourg's rule in the early 15th century. ⏱ *1–2 hr. 16/16A/116 to Dísz tér.*

② **Miró Café.** This necessarily colorful tribute to Catalan Surrealist artist Joan Miró is a fun contrast to the almost overpowering architecture of the Castle District. Known for its ice cream, breakfast and light lunch is also served. *Úri utca 30. At Dísz tér.* ☎ *1/201-5573. $$.*

The imposing and multi-faceted Royal Palace.

Ornate altar in St. Matthias Church.

3 ★★★ **St. Matthias Church.** Just a stone's throw away from the Fisherman's Bastion lies the mainly neo-Gothic St. Matthias Church (Mátyás Templom), which is topped off by an extraordinarily multi-colored tiled roof. While King Matthias Corvinus didn't build the church from scratch, he did extend and repair the then 200-year-old Gothic structure in the 15th century. He also made good use of it, having two of his three marriages there. Charles Robert was the first to be crowned here in 1308, while Charles IV was the last in 1916 and indeed the last Habsburg Monarch. In preparing for the millennium celebrations in 1896, Frigyes Schulek hacked away some of the 15th-century additions in a rather impressive bid to restore the church's original look. 19th-century artists Károly Lotz and Bertalan Székely bring Hungarian legends and history to life inside. I love the calm and soft tones of the interior, which is also one of the few places where the din of tourist chatter dies down, and the color of the roof gives something modern (well, it was cutting edge in 1896) to the neo-Gothic visage. ⏲ *30 min. Szentháromság tér 2.* ☎ *1/489-0716. Admission Ft 700. Free to pray. Bus 16/16A/116 to Dísz tér.*

4 **Equestrian Statue of King István.** Popping up right between Matthias Church and the Fisherman's Bastion, Hungary's first monarch reminds everyone who's boss in Hungary's story. He even stole King Matthias's thunder by putting the first church up here in 1015. The statue itself is the work of master sculptor Alajos Stróbl, but the altarpiece on which the statue rests is from Frigyes Schulek's design, hence the smooth integration with its two surrounding sights.

5 ★★★ **kids Fisherman's Bastion.** The seven Disney-like mini towers might look custom-built for Snow White's troupe, but the fact that there

Equestrian statue of King István.

are seven refers rather to the seven leaders of the Magyar tribes who galloped in to claim Hungary in 896 AD. This fairytale blend of neo-Gothic and neo-Romanesque, conjured up by Frigyes Schulek, affords stunning views over to Parliament and sprawling Pest. The steps that run down beside it were poorly guarded when the invading Turks piled in to seize the Castle.

🕐 *30 min. Admission Ft 400 to enter the towers but you can explore the lower parts for free.*

6️⃣ kids ★★★ Ruszwurm Cukrászda. Refuel over coffee with a green marzipan-topped Mátyás cake at this cute and cozy, still family-run Budapest institution (p 37, bullet ⓫). *Szentháromság utca 7.* ☎ *1/375-5284. $–$$.*

7️⃣ András Hadik's Equestrian Statue. Quite why it is that students from the nearby Engineering University consider it good luck before exams to rub the big brassy

The fairytale towers of the Fisherman's Bastion.

Statue of András Hadik and his lucky horse.

testicles of this Huszár's horse is anybody's guess, but it's one of the few remaining activities that's free in the Castle District. Hadik incidentally was a Slovak who rose to the high rank of commander in the Austrian army serving in the Seven Years War, even taking Berlin and serving as the protector of Buda Castle.

8️⃣ kids Cave Hospital and Bunker. The fascinating subterranean complex of 2,000 sq m/6,560 sq ft runs underneath the Castle and served as a World War II hospital and Cold War nuclear shelter. *Lovas út 4c. Admission Ft 3,000. 10am–6pm, closed Mon.*

9️⃣ kids Magdalene Tower. This large 13th-century Franciscan church was almost consigned to the history books by allied bombing in World War II, but the tower and a Gothic vaulted window obstinately rise out of the ghostly ruins thanks to reconstruction completed in 1997. In the early days of the Ottoman occupation, the Turks allowed Christians to use the church, bringing both Protestants and Catholics to worship here, but in different parts of the church, of course. Later it was converted into a mosque, returning to its former use after the Turks were expelled. *Kapisztrán tér.*

⑩ ★★★ **Explore the old cobbled streets between Táncsics Mihály utca and Tóth Árpád sétány.** These streets, slightly away from the madding tourist crowd, hold more fascination for me than the more famous sights. Here, you realize that the Castle District isn't just a museum-piece and that people do actually live in these cute houses, many of which date back to the 19th and 18th centuries, some earlier. On Táncsics Mihály utca, which was once part of the Jewish quarter, look out for the elaborate courtyard of former Erődy mansion at number 7, which is now home to the Music History Institute. Steeped in history itself, Beethoven once stayed here. On the same street, you can see houses that have been built on the original medieval foundations, such as number 10 with its upper niche containing a vase and shell. Fortuna utca features charming neo-classical and Baroque houses, while the triangle of houses on Országház utca at numbers 20, 22 and 5, directly opposite, feature a Gothic ledge with arch, a fabulous bay window, and a stunning gate, respectively. At 32 Úri utca, check out at the partly preserved Gothic sedilia next to the gate. Tóth Árpád sétány skirts around the perimeter of the inner Castle District and is great for a walk with a view.

⑪ ★★ **Bécsi kapu tér.** The 'Vienna Gate' is where the Hungarians finally overpowered the Turks to re-enter and reclaim the Castle in 1686, though the Vienna Gate that stands here today dates back to just

Great views from the Castle District.

1936 (see p 32, bullet ⑤). At the square's center, the fountain, which features a girl protecting a sacred light, is a tribute to writer Ferenc Kazinczy and his efforts to develop the Hungarian language in the 18th century when its usage was far from universal. Foreigners who are struggling with this seemingly impenetrable language at least have someone to blame. Kazinczy didn't have an easy time of it though and was sentenced to death for his role as a Jacobin along with the movement's leader Ignác Martinovics, priest of the Magdalene Church. Like the Hungarian language, but unlike Martinovics, Kazinczy survived. It seems fitting that the domineering National Archives building, with its colorfully tiled Zsolnay roof, overlooks the square. Substantially less imposing is the tiny Lutheran church on the opposite side of the square. Noted Greek and Roman guru József Grigely once lived at 7 Bécsi kapu tér, which accounts for the relief featuring Pallas Athena and Classical authors including the likes of Virgil and Socrates. *Bécsi kapu tér.* ●

Shopping Best Bets

Best **American Mall Experience**
★★ Arena Plaza, *Kerepesi út 9 (p 78)* and ★★ Westend City Center, *Váci út 1–3 (p 78)*

Best **Art Auction House**
★★★ Kieselbach, Szent István körút 5 (p 71) and ★★★ Virág Judit Mű-terem, *Falk Miksa utca 30 (p 72)*

Best **Bejing-style Market Experience**
★ Józsefvárosi Piac, *Kőbányai út 21–23 (p 76)*

Best **Ceramics**
★★★ Herend, József Nádor tér 11 (p 73) and ★★★ Zsolnay, *Váci utca 19–21 (p 73)*

Best for **Firewater**
★ Magyar Pálinka Háza (House of Hungarian Pálinka), *Rákóczi út 17 (p 80)* and ★★ Zwack Shop, *Soroksári út (p 80)*

Best **Flea Market**
★★★ Ecseri Piac, *Nagykörösi út 156 (p 76)*

Best **Food Market**
★★★ Great Market Hall, *Vámház körút 1–3 (p 77)*

Best **Funky Gifts**
★★ Szupernova, *Irányi utca 20 (p 73)* and ★★ Repülő Tehén, *Hajós utca (p 77)*

Best **Handmade Shoes**
★★ Vass Shoes, *Harris köz 2 (p 76)*

Best **Hats**
★★ V50 Design Art Studio, *Váci utca 50 (p 73)*

Best **Hungarian Designer**
★★★ Katti Zoób, *Szent István körút 17 (p 73)*

Best **Jewelry**
★★★ Wladis Galéria és Műterem, *Falk Miksa utca 13 (p 75)*

Best **Retro Magyar Sneakers**
★ Tisza Cipő, *Károly körút 1 (p 76)*

Best **Salami**
★★ Pick Márkaáruház, *Kossuth Lajos tér 9 (p 79)*

Best **Wine Shop**
★★ Bortársaság, *Batthyány utca 59 or Szent István tér 3 (p 80)*

Handmade footwear at Vass Shoes.

Buda Shopping

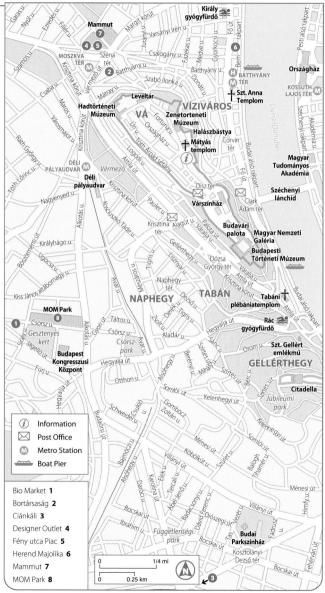

Information

(i) Information
⊠ Post Office
Ⓜ Metro Station
🚢 Boat Pier

Bio Market **1**
Bortársaság **2**
Ciánkáli **3**
Designer Outlet **4**
Fény utca Piac **5**
Herend Majolika **6**
Mammut **7**
MOM Park **8**

Central Pest Shopping

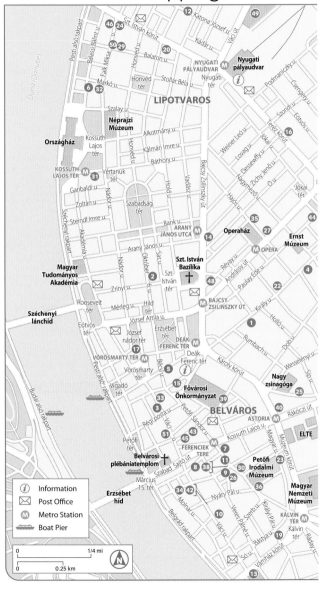

Information

Post Office

Metro Station

Boat Pier

0   1/4 mi

0   0.25 km

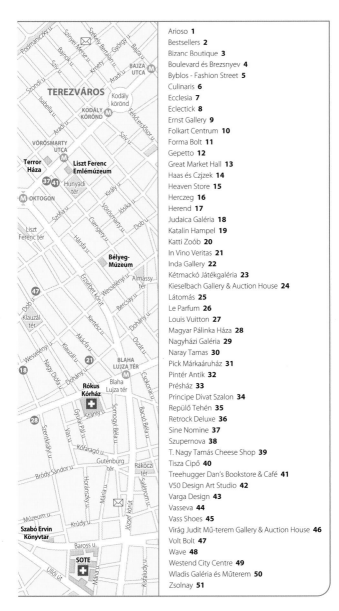

Outer Pest Shopping

Arena Plaza **1**
Ecseri Piac **2**
Fakopáncs **3**
Iguana **4**
Józsefvárosi Piac **5**
Monarchia **6**
PECSA Flea Market **7**
Zwack Shop **8**

⊠ Post Office
Ⓜ Metro Station
≋ Thermal Bath

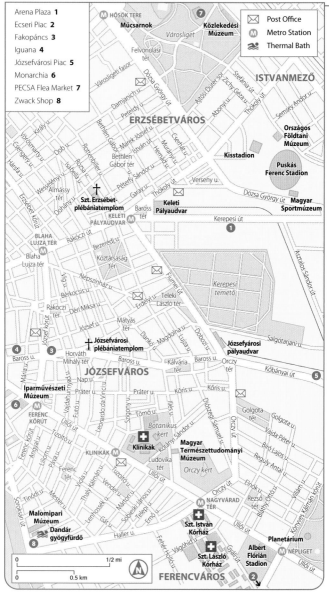

Budapest Shopping A to Z

Art & Antiques

★★★ Boulevard és Brezsnyev

CENTRAL PEST Cutting-edge paintings and objets d'art at reasonable prices from fledgling artists with innovative exhibitions opposite. Also sells vintage posters. *Király utca 39. (Temporary exhibitions: Király utca 46.)* ☎ *0630/944-5778. www.bbgaleria.hu. No credit cards. Metro: M1/M2/M3 to Deák tér. Tram: 4/6 to Király utca. Map p 68.*

★★ Ernst Gallery CENTRAL PEST

Charming gallery dealing in en vogue 'neglected' local artists; decorative and applied arts, plus Baroque, Biedermeier, Art Nouveau and Art Deco furniture. *Irányi utca 27 (corner of Cukor utca).* ☎ *1/266-4016 or 1/266-4017. www.ernstgaleria.hu. AE, MC, V. Metro: M3 to Ferenciek tere. Map p 68.*

★ Inda Gallery CENTRAL PEST

Located on arty Király utca but hidden away on the second floor of a townhouse, Inda offers paintings, installations, and sculptures from a talented younger generation. *Király utca 34 2/4 (corner of Székely Mihály utca).* ☎ *1/413-1960. www.inda galeria.hu. MC, V. Metro: M1/M2/M3 to Deák tér. Tram: 4/6 to Király utca. Map p 68.*

★★★ Kieselbach Gallery and Auction House CENTRAL PEST

This prestigious auction house, which marks the start of Pest's gallery-rich Falk Miksa utca, holds the world record for the auction of a Hungarian painting at $1.42 million for a Csontváry, who Picasso referred to as the other great painter of the 20th century. It also holds exhibitions. *Szent István körút 5 (corner of*

Ernst Gallery for Art Deco furniture and other treasures.

Falk Miksa utca). ☎ *1/269-3148 or 1/269-3149. www.kieselbach.hu. AE, DC, MC, V. Tram: 2/4/6 to Jászai Mari tér. Map p 68.*

★★ **Nagyházi Galéria** CENTRAL PEST Prominent auction house offering everything from paintings and sculpture to furniture, carpets, objets d'art, jewelry, folk art, and antiquities. *Balaton utca 8 (corner of Falk Miksa utca).* ☎ *1/475-6000 or 1/475-2090. www.nagyhazi.hu. AE, DC, MC, V. Tram: 2/4/6 to Jászai Mari tér. Map p 68.*

★ **Pintér Antik** CENTRAL PEST Huge selection of antiques, traditional and modern paintings, chandeliers, clocks, and sculpture for sale that is spread over 1,800 sq m/5,900 sq ft. Regular auctions. *Falk Miksa utca 10 (corner of Markó utca).* ☎ *1/311-3030. www.pinter antik.hu. MC, V. Tram: 2/4/6 to Jászai Mari tér. Map p 68.*

★★★ **Virág Judit Mű-terem Gallery and Auction House** CENTRAL PEST 19th- and 20th-century Hungarian paintings from big names in local art, including Munkácsy, Csontváry, and Rippl-Rónai, along with Art Nouveau ceramics from Zsolnay for sale and auction. *Falk Miksa utca 30.* ☎ *1/312-2071. www.mu-terem.hu. MC, V. Metro: M2 to Kossuth tér. Tram: 2/4/6 to Jászai Mari tér. Map p 68.*

Books (English Language)
★ **Bestsellers** CENTRAL PEST Although Bestsellers has plenty of healthy competition these days, its multi-genre selection of new English language books is hard to beat. Also great for newspapers and magazines. *Október 6. utca 11.* ☎ *1/312-1295. www.bestsellers.hu. AE, DC, MC, V. Metro: M3 to Arany János utca. Map p 68.*

Treehugger Dan's Bookstore & Café.

★ **Treehugger Dan's Bookstore & Café** CENTRAL PEST Choose a used paperback with a cup of Fairtrade coffee. Regular readings hosted. *Csengery utca 48.* ☎ *1/322-0774. www.treehugger.hu. No credit cards. Metro: M1 to Oktogon. Tram: 4/6 to Oktogon. (Branches: Lázár utca 6, Sütő utca 2.) Map p 68.*

Ceramics
★ **Haas és Czjzek** CENTRAL PEST Look out for Hollóháza with its funky Four Seasons design featuring a woman's face in each season, as well as plates from Alföldi (that serve many restaurants) plus Herend and Zsolnay. *Bajcsy Zsilinszky út 23 (corner of Zichy Jenő utca).* ☎ *1/311-4094. AE, MC, V. Cards. Metro: M3 to Arany János utca. Map p 68.*

★★★ **Herend** CENTRAL PEST From tasteful and intricate traditional items to light and breezy, Herend's legendary porcelain is always classy, and Queen Victoria was among its fans. A national treasure, albeit a pricey one. *József Nádor tér 11.* ☎ *1/317-2622. www.herend.com. AE, DC, MC, V. Metro: M1 to Vörösmarty tér. (Branch: Andrássy út 17.) Map p 68.*

Herend Village Pottery BUDA More cute and colorful, easy-going country-style designs from Hungary's renowned ceramics producer—still handmade—without breaking the bank. *Bem rakpart 37 (between Vitéz utca and Csalogány utca).* ☎ *1/356-7899. www.herend majolika.hu. AE, MC, V. Metro: M2 to Batthyány tér. Map p 67.*

★★★ **Zsolnay** CENTRAL PEST Zsolnay's colorful and super-durable pyrogranite tiles adorn the roofs of some of Budapest's most spectacular buildings. Its iridescent eosin technology also makes unique ceramics. *Váci utca 19–21 (corner of Párizsi utca).* ☎ *1/266-6305. MC, V. Metro: M3 to Ferenciek tere. Map p 68.*

Design
★ **Forma Bolt** CENTRAL PEST You never know when a plastic duck or frog-shaped bottle opener will come in handy. Come here for these and other wacky items. *Ferenciek tere 4.* ☎ *1/266-5053. www.forma.co.hu. MC, V. Metro: M3 to Ferenciek tere. Map p 68.*

★★ **Gepetto** CENTRAL PEST International award- winning, sleek minimalist interior design from sofas and shelves to kitchen furniture and lamps . Also some objects like the award-winning egg holder, should you wish to add a unique touch of authentic contemporary Budapest design to your home. *Katona József utca 15.* ☎ *1/270-0107. www. gepetto.hu. No credit cards. Metro: M3 to Nyugati pu. Tram: 4/6 to Nyugati pu. Map p 68.*

★★ **Szupernova** CENTRAL PEST Fun and colorful contemporary and retro interior design objects from

Hungarian and international designers. Look out for the groovy tin robots, plastic rabbits, and golden ducks. *Downstairs from Eclectick. Irányi utca 20.* ☎ *0620/828-9327. www.szupernova.hu. MC, V. Metro: M3 to Ferenciek tere. Map p 68.*

Fashion—Hats
★★ **V50 Design Art Studio** CENTRAL PEST Not quite as daring as Philip Treacy, but Valéria Fazekas's designer hats are wearable yet guaranteed to turn heads. Look out for her city-themed collection. *Váci utca 50.* ☎ *1/ 3375-320. No credit cards. Metro: M3 to Ferenciek tere. (Branch: Belgrád rakpart 16.) Map p 68.*

Fashion—Hungarian Designers
★★ **Eclectick** CENTRAL PEST Funky, cool but playful clothes and accessories from Eclectick, plus other Hungarian labels like Aquanauta, Camou, Heart and Roll, Red Aster, PUCC, and Kriszta Marosi. *Irányi utca 20 (corner of Károlyi Mihály utca).* ☎ *1/266-3341. www.eclectick. MC, V. Metro: M3 to Ferenciek tere. Map p 68.*

Unique ceramics from Zsolnay.

Herczeg CENTRAL PEST With a bit of a rock 'n' roll feel and a touch of metrosexuality to it, Zoltán Herczeg's checked and torn trousers, sleeveless shirts, and printed T-shirts are for guys who want to turn heads. *Teréz körút 35.* ☎ *0620/973-0443. No credit cards. Metro: M3 to Nyugati pu. M1 to Oktogon. Tram: 4/6 to Oktogon. Map p 68.*

★★★ **Katti Zoób** CENTRAL PEST Internationally acclaimed Katti Zoób creates flowing and classy feminine designs from top Italian fabrics, as well as distinctive jewelry and accessories using Zsolnay ceramics. Lacy and embroidered fine details appear in her haute couture range. *Szent István körút 17.* ☎ *1/312-1865. www.kattizoob.hu. MC, V. Metro: M3 to Nyugati pu. Tram: 2/4/6 to Jászai Mari tér. Map p 68.*

Látomás CENTRAL PEST   Upcoming designers like Kati Nádasdi, Zuppa, Lollypopp, and Balkán Tangó at bargain prices, although you might find yourself wading through some garish items before finding a gem. *Dohány utca 16–18.* ☎ *1/266-5052. www.latomas.hu. MC, V. Metro: M2 to Astoria. Tram: 47/49. Map p 68.*

★ **Naray Tamas** CENTRAL PEST   All that glitters is not gold in this Francophile designer Tamás Náray's chichi showroom in the Ybl Palace. Perhaps not using the best fabric expected of a famous designer you might just stumble upon the dress of your life. *Károlyi Mihály utca 12.* ☎ *1/266-2473. www.naray company.hu. AE, MC, V. Metro: M3 to Ferenciek tere. Map p 68.*

★ **Retrock Deluxe** CENTRAL PEST   A turn-of-the-century salon turned into a madhouse of crazy works by young Hungarian designers. Brand

Colorful Hungarian design at Eclectick.

names like Nanushka, Use Unused, Tamara Barnuff, Je Suiss Belle, Anh Tuan. *Henszlman Imre utca 1.* ☎ *0630/556-2814. No credit cards. Metro: M3 to Ferenciek tere. Map p 68.*

★★ **Sine Nomine** CENTRAL PEST   A shop showcasing talented young Hungarian designers exuding as much taste as the feminine dresses, beautiful knitwear, and accessories. *Andrássy út 57 (between Eötvös and Csengery utca).* ☎ *0620/959-9444. MC, V. Metro: M1 to Vörösmarty tér or Oktogon. Map p 68.*

★★ **Vasseva** CENTRAL PEST   A cute little shop on a side street off Liszt Ferenc tér selling Éva Vass's creations and interior décor items. Original ideas are combined with interesting materials, and the result is wearable clothes but with the edge you would expect from a costume designer, stylist, and artist. *Paulay Ede utca 67.* ☎ *1/342-8159. No credit cards. Metro: M1 to Oktogon. Tram: 4/6. Map p 68.*

Fashion—International Designers

★★ **Byblos—Fashion Street** CENTRAL PEST   Film producer Andy Vajna opened this exclusive 600 sq m/1,970 sq ft shop in 2007 selling Byblos, Byblos Blu, and some Rocco Barocco clothes and accessories. *Deák Ferenc utca 17 (corner of Bécsi utca).* ☎ *1/337-1908. AE, MC, V. Metro: M1/M2/M3 to Deák tér. Map p 68.*

Designer Outlet BUDA   Quality never goes out of fashion even if it's a few seasons behind. Two hundred new items arrive every Thursday from the likes of Ralph Lauren, DKNY, Roberto Cavalli, and Mark Jacobs at approaching bargain prices. *Lövőház utca 12 (Fény utca Piac).* ☎ *1/345-4133. AE, M, V.*

Drop by Iguana for Secondhand clothes and accessories.

Metro: M2 to Moszkva tér. Tram: 4/6 to Széna tér. Map p 67.

★★★ **Heaven Store** CENTRAL PEST The first high-flying multibrand store in Budapest offering personal appointments and a good selection of brands including Patrizia Pepe, Replay, Chloé, G-Star Raw, and Stella McCartney among others. *Fehérhajó utca 12–14.* ☎ *1/266-8335. www.heavenstore. hu. AE, DC, MC, V. Metro: M1/M2/M3 to Deák tér. Map p 68.*

★★ **Louis Vuitton** CENTRAL PEST Just a few steps away from the opera house this exclusive shop offers a stunning collection of bags and suitcases for those who know the difference between a real and a fake LV bag. *Andrássy út 24.* ☎ *1/373-0487. AE, DC, MC, V. Metro: M1 to Opera. Map p 68.*

★★★ **Principe Divat Szalon** CENTRAL PEST A good selection of the latest collection of luxury brands such as Dolce & Gabbana, John Galliano, Just Cavalli, and Ferre. Plus, if you're lucky, you might find something on sale. *Váci utca 50 (corner of Nyári Pál utca).* ☎ *1/318-1119. www.principe.hu. AE, M, V. Metro: M3 to Ferenciek tere. Map p 68.*

Fashion—Jewelry
★★ **Varga Design** CENTRAL PEST Handmade jewelry based on Miklós Varga's patented approach to imitate the image of sun reflecting on dewdrops collecting on a cobweb. Like a spider's web, each item is unique. *Haris Köz 6.* ☎ *1/318-4089. www.vargadesign.hu. AE, DC, MC, V. Metro: M3 to Ferenciek tere. Map p 68.*

★★★ **Wladis Galéria és Műterem** CENTRAL PEST Peter Vladimir's original jewelry reflects traditional and ancient designs. Chunky but classy sculpted pieces made from quality silver with rings starting from around Ft 20,000, necklaces about Ft 30,000. *Falk Miksa utca 13 (corner of Balaton utca).* ☎ *1/354-0834. www.wladis galeria.hu. MC, V. Tram: 2/4/6 to Jászai Mari tér. Map p 68.*

Fashion—Secondhand
Ciánkáli OUTER BUDA The largest stock of retro vintage clothes is quite a way from downtown but you're sure to find something that will still set contemporary pulses racing. *Repülőtéri út 6. 8/D.* ☎ *0630/456-7018. www.majomke trec.hu. MC, V. Tram: 41 to Repülőtér. Map p 67.*

Iguana CENTRAL PEST If it's a Jesus or Elvis T-shirt you're missing, pop in to Iguana. Mainly secondhand clothes, shoes, and retro accessories for sale. *Krúdy Gyula utca 9.* ☎ *1/317-1627. www.iguana retro.hu. No credit cards. Metro: M3 to Kálvin tér. Tram: 4/6. (Branch: Tompa utca 1.* ☎ *1/215-3475.) Map p 70.*

Fashion—Shoes

★★ Bizanc Boutique CENTRAL PEST
The best assortment of the season's designer shoes for men and women from Jimmy Choo, John Richmond, Moschino, Anna Sui, Giuseppe Zanotti, GML, and more, with handbags to match. Fur and leather coats, too. *Váci utca 9.* ☎ *1/317-8368. AE, MC, V . Metro: M1 to Vörösmarty tér. M2/M3 to Deák tér. Map p 68.*

★ Tisza Cipő CENTRAL PEST
Retro sneakers with the trademark 'T' on each design from Hungary's very own casual shoemaker. Also, look out for funky tops and jackets. There's another store in the Westend shopping mall (see p 78). *Károly körút 1 (corner of Rákóczi út).* ☎ *1/266-3055. www.tiszacipo.hu. AE, MC, V. Metro: M2 to Astoria. Tram: 47/49 to Astoria. Map p 68.*

★★ Vass Shoes CENTRAL PEST
Handmade shoes that fit perfectly, boast amazing quality of material and precise craftsmanship. László Vass has managed to turn the old traditional shoemaking profession into a modern business. *Harris köz 2.* ☎ *1/318-2375. www.vass-cipo.hu. AE, DC, MC, V. Metro: M3 to Ferenciek tere. Map p 68.*

Flea Markets

★★★ Ecseri Piac OUTER PEST
Remarkable flea market packed with some quality antiques and no end of Socialist-era bric-à-brac. Paintings, furniture, soda siphons, rocking horses, Zsolnay ceramics, old motorbikes, even antique BMW bubble cars: it's all there. Bargaining expected. *Nagykörösi út 156.* ☎ *1/348-3200. Bus: 54 to Alvinc utca. Map p 70.*

★ Józsefvárosi Piac OUTER PEST
While the bottom is likely to fall out of the jeans you buy quicker than it takes you to walk around this sprawling Chinese market, it feels pretty close to being in China. Good Chinese food. *Kőbányai út 21–23.* ☎ *1/313-8890. Tram: 28 to Orczy tér. Map p 70.*

★ PECSA Flea Market OUTER PEST
With the abundance of fake brands, chunky transistor radios, Russian dolls, medals, and so on, I feel momentarily transported back to pre-1989 Budapest when I visit this market. Open mornings at the weekend. *Zichy Mihály utca.* ☎ *1/363-3730. Metro: M1 to Széchenyi fürdő. Map p 70.*

Bric-a-brac at Ecseri Piac flea market.

Flowers

★★ Arioso CENTRAL PEST

Creative arrangements verging on designer, and just the ticket if you've been invited to dinner. Much more than flowers, Arioso is also an interior designer. *Király utca 9.* 🕿 *1/266-3555. www.arioso.hu. Closed first 3 weeks of Aug. AE, MC, V. Metro: M1/M2/M3 to Deák tér. Map p 68.*

Folk Art

★ Folkart Centrum CENTRAL PEST

Folk art products including embroidered tablecloths, painted dolls, and ceramics for those who don't want to haggle in return for guaranteed quality from serious artisans. *Váci utca 58.* 🕿 *1/318-4697. AE, DC, MC, V. Metro: M3 to Ferenciek tere. Map p 68.*

Folkart Centrum.

Katalin Hampel CENTRAL PEST Hungarian and European folk costumes adapted 'for the modern woman', although some outfits, as well as the menswear, are more the preserve of period ballgoers. *Királyi Pál utca 11.* 🕿 *0620/597-0893. No credit cards. Metro: M3 to Kálvin tér. Map p 68.*

Food Markets

★ Bio Market BUDA

Taste just how fresh Hungarian fruit and veg can be at this Saturday morning organic produce extravaganza that runs from 6am to noon or 1pm should there be enough shoppers. The fruit juices are sublime. *Csörsz utca 18.* 🕿 *1/214-7005. No credit cards. Tram: 61 to Csörsz utca. Map p 67.*

★ Fény utca piac BUDA

Made from 1970s-style iron and girders, this neighborhood market lacks the fin-de-siècle charm of some of its peers, but makes up for it in the range of Hungarian agricultural produce. For fine cheese, hams, and salami head to the top level. *Lövőház utca 12.* 🕿 *1/345-4101. Metro: M2 to Moszkva tér. Tram: 4/6 to Széna tér. Map p 67.*

★★★ Great Market Hall CENTRAL PEST

Aside from the architecture (see p 17, bullet ③) this is a great place to pick up 'Hungaricums' like powdered paprika, tubes of paprika paste, tins of chestnut puree, and goose liver. Plenty of painted folk art and tablecloths, too. *Vámház körút 1–3.* 🕿 *1/366-3300. Credit cards not widely used. Tram: 2/47/49 to Fővám tér. Map p 68.*

Funky Gifts

★★ Repülő Tehén (Flying Cow) CENTRAL PEST

The 'Flying Cow' is jammed with zany gifts from seriously cool pink grinning Buddhas to Geisha ashtrays, funky fridge magnets, Playboy bottle openers, and cheeky 'naked' mugs. *Hajós utca 19.* 🕿 *0620/204-5574. www.repulotehen.hu. MC, V. Metro: M1 to Opera. (Branch: Mammut Shopping Mall.) Map p 68.*

★ Volt Bolt CENTRAL PEST

Cool T-shirts and accessories from the organizers of the Sziget Festival, Budapest's mega music festival, many of which relate to the Sziget or other festivals. *Klauzál tér 14 (corner of Akácfa utca).* 🕿 *0620/385-0827. www.voltbolt.hu. MC, V. Tram: 4/6 to Király utca. Map p 68.*

The Best Shopping

Malls

★★ kids Arena Plaza OUTER PEST

Just when Budapest seemed to reach saturation point with mega malls, along came Arena Plaza with more space and brands than anybody else, plus the first IMAX cinema in Hungary, replete with VIP booths. *Kerepesi út 9.* ☎ *1/880-7000. www.arenaplaza.hu. Metro: M2 to Keleti Pu or Stadionok. Map p 70.*

★ kids Mammut BUDA

Divided into two main parts: Mammut 1 and 2, Mammut, i.e. mammoth, never gets too overwhelming in proportions and is more easy-going than Westend (see below) but still packed with shops. The roof level of Mammut 2 is home to a Gold's Gym. *Lövőház utca 2–6.* ☎ *1/345-8020. www.mammut.hu. Metro: M2 to Moszkva tér. Tram: 4/6 to Széna tér. Map p 67.*

★★ kids MOM Park BUDA

Spacious and modern mall, home to the only Budapest branch of high-end children's clothes specialist Jacadi, gourmet food shops, popular Italian restaurant Dallello, and the Bavarian Paulaner Brauhaus beer hall (see p 119). *Alkotás utca 53.* ☎ *1/487-5500. www.mompark.hu. Tram: 61 to MOM Park. Map p 67.*

★★ kids Westend City Center CENTRAL PEST

You could be fooled into thinking you're in a big American mall here—that is until sub-standard Hungarian service reminds you you're in Hungary. Busy and popular with a huge number of Hungarian and international brands to choose from. *Váci út 1–3.* ☎ *1/238-7777. www.westend.hu. Metro: M3 to Nyugati pu. Tram: 4/6 to Nyugati pu. Map p 68.*

Music

★★ Wave CENTRAL PEST

Run by an affable music lover, who I often run into at gigs, Wave is stacked with Hungarian and international alternative, indie, dance, ethno, and jazz CDs, DVDs, and LPs that are hard to find elsewhere. *Révay utca 4.* ☎ *1/331-0781. No credit cards. Metro: M3 to Arany János utca. Map p 68.*

Perfumes

★★ Le Parfum CENTRAL PEST

Custom-made fragrances from the philosophical and talented French-educated perfumer Zsolt Zólyomi. Also, limited edition high-end perfumes from the likes of Burberry, Bottega Veneta, and Clive Christian. *Cukor utca 1.* ☎ *0630/470-0248. No*

Fresh Hungarian fruit at the Bio Market.

back home. Also good for Magyar specialties. Impressive wine selection. *Balassi Bálint utca 7.* ☎ *1/373-0028. www.culinaris.hu. AE, MC, V. Tram: 2/4/6 to Jászai Mari tér. Branches: Hunyadi tér 3 & Perc utca 8. Map p 68.*

★★ **Pick Márkaáruház** CENTRAL PEST   Although you'll see Pick's definitive téliszalámi 'winter' salami all over town, this shop stocks many other delicious Pick salamis, some spicy others smooth, and other meat products. Cafeteria upstairs. *Kossuth Lajos tér 9.* ☎ *1/331-7783. No credit cards. Metro: M2 to Kossuth Lajos tér. Tram: 2 to Kossuth Lajos tér. Map p 68.*

★ **T. Nagy Tamás Cheese Shop** CENTRAL PEST   Outstanding ensemble of Hungarian and international cheeses, particularly French. Although Hungary is less renowned for cheese, look out for the excellent local goat cheese. *Gerlóczy utca 3.* ☎ *1/317-4268. MC, V. Metro: M1/M2/M3 to Deák tér. Map p 68.*

Culinaris for international foodstuffs.

Jewish gifts and art at Judaica Galéria.

credit cards. Metro: M3 to Ferenciek tere. Map p 68.

Religious
Ecclesia CENTRAL PEST   Next to a pretty Franciscan church, this is the place to come for religious objects and hand-painted religious icons from Hungary and further east. *Ferenciek tere 7.* ☎ *1/317-3061. MC, V. Metro: M3 to Ferenciek tere. Map p 68.*

★★ **Judaica Galéria** CENTRAL PEST   Teddy bears wearing kippas (skullcaps), Dead Sea beauty treatments, and recipe books feature among the eclectic Jewish gift items. It also serves as a serious Jewish arts gallery and auction house. *Wesselényi utca 13.* ☎ *1/ 267-8502. MC, V. Metro: M2 to Astoria. Map p 68.*

Specialty Foods
★★ **Culinaris** CENTRAL PEST   Packed out with hungry expats relishing the range of international foodstuffs that they take for granted

Toys

★★★ Fakopáncs

CENTRAL PEST Creative Hungarian-made wooden toys to make kids think beyond the realm of the X-box and Barbie doll. Excellent for gifts and with a flawless safety record, too. *József körút 50.* ☎ *1/333-1866. www.fakopancs.com. No credit cards. Tram: 4 or 6 to Baross utca. (Branches inc. Baross utca 46.) Map p 70.*

★★ Kétmackó Játékgaléria

CENTRAL PEST Old-fashioned puppets and dolls, wooden toys, and game-themed paintings are on sale along with skill-enhancing activity and board games at the 'Two Bears Toy Gallery'. *Magyar utca 18.* ☎ *1/266-0928. www.ketmacko.hu. No credit cards. Metro: M2 to Astoria. Map p 68.*

Wine & Spirits

★★ Bortársaság (Wine Society)

BUDA Strong selection of Hungarian wines from most Hungarian regions with knowledgeable staff on hand. Other branches include one opposite St. Stephen's Basilica at Szent István tér 3. *Batthyány utca 59.* ☎ *1/212-2569. www.bortarsasag.hu. AE, MC, V. Metro: M2 to Moszkva tér. Tram: 4/6 to Széna tér. Map p 67.*

★★ In Vino Veritas

CENTRAL PEST More old-fashioned looking than the slick Bortársaság (see above), Veritas also represents an impressive batch of quality-driven Hungarian winemakers. *Dohány utca 58–62.* ☎ *1/341-3174 or*

Pálinka fruit brandy bottles.

1/341-0646. www.borkereskedes.hu. MC, V. Metro: M2 to Astoria. Tram: 47/49 to Astoria. Map p 68.

★ Magyar Pálinka Háza (House of Hungarian Pálinka)

CENTRAL PEST Comprehensive collection of Hungary's fruit brandy known as Pálinka, now an EU-protected name. Pálinka ranges from the seriously fiery to the soft and fruity. *Rákóczi út 17.* ☎ *1/338-4219. MC, V. Metro: M2 to Blaha Lujza tér. Map p 68.*

★ Monarchia

CENTRAL PEST Monarchia sells its own range of wines made in Eger by the talented winemaker Tamás Pók that are exported to the US. Also represents Hungarian and boutique international wineries. *Kinizsi utca 30–36.* ☎ *1/456-9898. www.monarchiaborok.hu. AE, MC, V. Metro: M3 to Ferenc körút. Tram: 4/6 to Ferenc körút. Map p 70.*

Présház

CENTRAL PEST A wine shop on touristy Váci utca would normally make me wary, but this is a good one, selling a wide range of Hungarian wines plus some vintages of top labels, long since sold out elsewhere. *Váci utca 10.* ☎ *1/266-1100. www.preshaz.hu. MC, V. Metro: M1 to Vörösmarty tér. Map p 68.*

★★ Zwack Shop

OUTER PEST Zwack makes the ubiquitous bitter Hungarian liqueur Unicum that you'll either love or hate. I prefer the deliciously fruity Nemes Pálinka (fruit brandy) range and its boutique wine range. *Soroksári út 26.* ☎ *1/476-2383. www.zwack.hu. AE, MC, V. Tram: 2 to Haller utca. Map p 70.* ●

5 The Best **of the Outdoors**

City **Park**

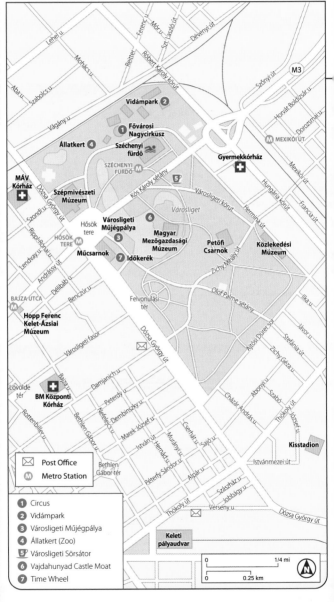

⊠	Post Office
Ⓜ	Metro Station

1 Circus
2 Vidámpark
3 Városligeti Műjégpálya
4 Állatkert (Zoo)
5' Városligeti Sörsátor
6 Vajdahunyad Castle Moat
7 Time Wheel

0   1/4 mi
0   0.25 km

This oasis of green is flanked by a multitude of old-fashioned attractions including a circus, a zoo, and an amusement park that features Europe's longest wooden rollercoaster that will remind Western travelers of the more innocent time they grew up in. START: **M1 to Széchenyi Fürdő. All the points of interest are served by the Széchenyi Fürdő metro station but everything is also accessible from the Heroes Square (Hősök tere) metro station.**

The old-style Vidámpark.

❶ ★★★ kids **Circus.** Lions, tigers, and bears, and elephants, too. However, this 120-year-old Budapest institution seeks to embrace the age of animal rights with an increasing reliance on its talented human performers. Three different troupes feature classic circus performances from clowns, acrobats, trapeze artists, and tightrope walkers. 🕐 *1 hr 30 min. Állatkerti*

körút 12/a. ☎ *1/343-8300. www. maciva.hu. Admission Ft 1,200– Ft 2,400. Performances Wed–Sun (excluding Sep). More performances at weekends.*

❷ ★★★ kids **Vidámpark (Amusement Park).** Passing by, it looks a sorry excuse for an amusement park but step in and you're transported back to a charming, old-fashioned world of well-kept and

Classic Courtyards—Behind the City's Grand Façades

As you're walking around the downtown do look out for open doorways of the magnificent buildings and have a peek in. Each of Budapest's stunning Habsburg-era townhouses, and there are many, tell their own story on the inside where they really come to life. If you get stuck, there's always a button to press that lets you out.

Hidden City Squares

While peace and quiet is harder to find in Pest than it is in leafy Buda, you don't have to trek out to City Park or Margaret Island to experience what is known as 'park life' as a secluded spot is often never more than a few corners away. The cute park at **Honvéd tér** with its trimmed lawn and neat flowerbeds is tucked away close to the busy Pest thoroughfare of Szent István körút but is totally peaceful, bar the sounds of kids playing. There's also concrete ping-pong tables with iron nets that may be an unglamorous hangover from Communism but they can stand all weather and make for a good game. You'll run into English speakers here and also on the playgrounds of **Szabadság tér**. Although Szabadság tér, literally Freedom Square, may be synonymous with the violence after the riots of 2006 (see p 47, bullet ③) and repression in the form of the Soviet War Memorial, this big open space, surrounded by colossal buildings that serve to block out the bustle, is a superbly relaxing place and you can contemplate the awesome aspect of the city's bigger-than-thou architecture. Still on the Pest side, **Károly kert** also belies its central location close to hectic Astoria, transcending metropolitan modernity and transporting you back to Budapest's early 20th-century heyday. Step through the wrought-iron gate and feel at the center of a living bastion of old-world charm.

restored attractions. Among the star attractions is the centegenarian wooden merry-go-round, which churns out swirlingly authentic Wurlitzer music—you have to ride the horses to keep the old girl moving. Budapest's 'Happy Park' boasts the longest wooden rollercoaster in Europe, which is nice to ride compared with more modern versions. The laser dodgems show that the park is not entirely stuck in the past. Go-karting costs an extra Ft 600 a go. Take toddlers of 3 and under to the mini amusement park that's attached. You'll find

playgrounds for younger infants within the City Park. It also has an interesting pay-according-to-height entry policy. ⏱ *2–3 hr. Állatkerti körút 14–16.* ☎ *1/363-8310. www. vidampark.hu. Ft 3,900 for people over 140cm, 100cm–140cm Ft 2,900, free for under 100cm. Daily Jun & Aug 10am–8pm, May–Sep 11am–7pm, mid-Mar–Oct 12am–6pm. Closed early Nov–mid-Mar.*

③ ★★★ kids
Városligeti Műjég-pálya (City Park Ice Rink). As the chill of winter hits, the fairy-tale atmosphere of the ice rink, with a pavilion on one side and the

Monkey about at the zoo.

Rowing on Vajdahunyad Castle Moat.

Vajdahunyad Castle (p 13, bullet ②) on the other, keeps the locals coming to the City Park. Gliding along the ice—or, if you're anything like me, falling over—is quite an experience with the Castle looming above. No need to worry about global warming here, just remember to wrap up well. 🕐 *2 hr. Olof Palme sétány 5.* ☎ *1/364-0013. www.mujegpalya.hu. Ft 700 per session weekdays, Ft 970 on weekends. Mon–Fri 9am–1pm, 4pm–8pm. Metro: M1 to Hősök tere.*

④ kids ★★ Állatkert (Zoo).

The first time I came here in the 1990s I felt indignant when I saw the cramped conditions and the sorry-looking, stir-crazy elephants. However, credit where credit's due, this place has become much more animal-friendly and is a nice place to bring the family to monkey about. I'm fascinated with the big rock that looks just like the one out of Spielberg's *Close Encounters* and the domain of gorillas and orangutans. Kids will also love the petting zoo. The Art Nouveau entrance, with its Oriental and Indian aspects and fine animal carvings and sculptures, is a suitably impressive teaser for what's inside. 🕐 *2 hr. Állatkerti körút 6–12.* ☎ *1/273-4900. www.zoobudapest. com. Admission Ft 1,690. 9am–7pm in summer. 9am–6pm in winter.*

⑤ Városligeti Sörsátor.

An old-fashioned beer tent bang in the right place, in the middle of the park, just when you need it. Ideal for a sausage (kolbász), pretzels (perec), or the savory scone known as pogácsa. For a more Boho setting head to Kertem (see p 123). *Városligeti Sétány.* ☎ *1/363-1904. $.*

⑥ kids Row in the Vajdahunyad Castle Moat.

It may be a folly and an eclectic mix of Hungarian architectural styles across the ages, but the Vajdahunyad Castle sure makes an attractive backdrop for a spot of easy rowing. Pick up a boat opposite the Castle entrance. 🕐 *30 min–1 hr. No phone. Ft 700 ½ hr, Ft 1,300 1 hr.*

⑦ kids Időkerék (Time Wheel).

Unveiled as Hungary entered a new epoch in joining the EU on May 1, 2004, public interest in this, one of the world's largest hourglasses, has dwindled. However, this clock isn't built for short-term hype. It doesn't actually tell the time but it is an impressive fusion of ancient techniques and state-of-the-art technology that's built to last the ravages of time. *Behind the Műcsarnok.*

Buda **Hills**

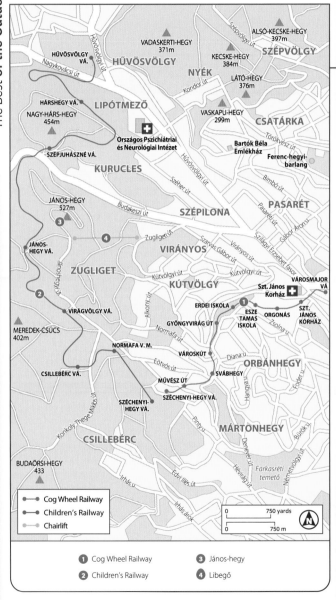

- ●——● Cog Wheel Railway
- ●——● Children's Railway
- ●——● Chairlift

0 — 750 yards
0 — 750 m

1 Cog Wheel Railway   **3** János-hegy

2 Children's Railway   **4** Libegő

Budapest is hardly a small city and has a population of around 2 million. However, I love the fact that you get up to the fresh air of the hills within minutes. This 'best of the hills' route provides a sampler but I encourage you to jump off wherever the mood takes you. START: **Tram 56 to Városmajor to connect with the Cog Wheel Railway to start your ascent.**

① kids **Ride the Fogaskerekű (Cog Wheel Railway).** The route to the Buda Hills is gradual but the feeling of being dragged up at an angle as the city starts to give way to more and more green certainly sets the tone. Take the cog to Széchenyi hegy where you can connect with the Children's Railway (bullet **②**) by walking along Golfpálya utca. *Tram: 56 to Városmajor. The service now runs under the number 60 according to the Budapest Public Transport Company. Runs from 5am–11:10pm.*

② kids ★★★ **Gyermekvasút (Children's Railway).** There's nothing like running a railway for instilling discipline and that was the philosophy behind the founding of this narrow gauge railway, once run by pioneers, a kind of Communist youth initiative. Included among the ranks of the pioneers is the current

Ride the Cog Wheel Railway.

Socialist Prime Minister, Ferenc Gyurcsány. Today children still run the show, although like in the past, I'm relieved to know that adults actually drive the trains and do the signaling. However, I do find it reassuring how seriously these kids take their jobs. It's a great way of traversing the Buda Hills and I recommend you just jump off wherever takes your fancy; otherwise continue to János hegy. Be warned, don't mess with these kids, they're stricter than adults—who knows what they'll do if you don't buy a ticket. A steam engine runs at weekends (p 39, bullet **③**). ⏲ *17 min to János hegy. Széchenyi hegy. Ft 450 one way.*

③ kids ★★ **János-hegy.** Budapest's highest point is topped off by the Erzsébet lookout tower. It's the work of that man Schulek again, he of Fisherman's Bastion (p 62) fame and renovator of St. Matthias (p 62), and you'll certainly see his signatory dreaminess here. ⏲ *30 min.*

④ ★★ **Libegő.** Hang on and be whisked down 262m/860ft from János hegy through the forest by this clunky but cool chairlift. Although it's not specifically a ski lift, crafty locals will take their skis up to the top on it when there's snow. Alternatively, you could also ascend this way to reach János hegy from the terminus at Zugligeti út 97. ⏲ *15 min.* ☎ *1/391-0352. Ft 500 one way. Bus: 155 to Zugligeti út.*

Margaret **Island**

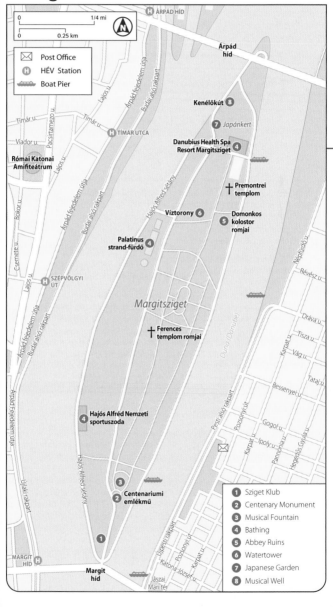

0 | 1/4 mi
0 | 0.25 km

⊠ Post Office
Ⓗ HÉV Station
🚢 Boat Pier

1 Sziget Klub
2 Centenary Monument
3 Musical Fountain
4 Bathing
5 Abbey Ruins
6 Watertower
7 Japanese Garden
8 Musical Well

Leafy **Margaret Island (Margitsziget) is a haven for morning runners** and midnight lovers. Located minutes from the downtown in the middle of the mighty Danube between Buda and Pest, locals come to escape the traffic and bustle of the city. It has also become an increasingly good place to party, now that an array of fun summer outdoor venues have sprung up. What would saintly Princess Margit (Margaret)—given to God by her father, Béla IV, for sparing his country from the Mongols—make of all the hedonism on her hallowed island? While people flock here in summer, I find it much more tranquil and idyllic in the winter months, especially when fresh snow falls. START: **Tram 4/6 to Margitsziget or take bus 26 which stops at several points on the island and you can hop on and off as you wish.**

1 ★★ **Sziget Klub.** Entering from the central Margit híd, after about 100m on the left you come to my favorite tennis club. It may say 'Only for Members', but if they have a court free you'll get a game; sadly it's the only remaining tennis club on the island. There's also a plunge pool in which to soak tired bones after a hard game. Recently renovated from its former high-end Socialist retro look, the clubhouse now has more of a lounge room feel. Either way, it's still a lovely place to play tennis and also has a new summer terrace bar that opened in summer 2008 (see Best Nightlife, p 123). ☎ *0620/420-7333. Bring your own rackets.*

2 **Centenary Monument.** Carry on straight and you'll be greeted by the twisty Centenary Monument whose intertwining symbolism represents the fusion of Buda and Pest. It has stood on this spot since 1972

Locals lazing around the Musical Fountain.

when it marked a hundred years since Budapest became one entity.

3 kids **Musical Fountain.** A bit further on you'll come to the curious spectacle of the musical fountain, which really requires no explanation other than it spurts out classical music intermittently. The spray carried by the breeze on to

Hajógyári-sziget

'Boatyard Island' is the next island upriver from Margaret Island and has big green open spaces that are given over to the Sziget Festival for one week each year (see p 161). It's also home to some of the capital's glitziest nightclubs (see Nightlife p 109). For golf enthusiasts, there's also a driving range.

A River Runs Through It— the River Danube

The banks of the mighty but murky Danube tend to be dominated by roads, but the stretch on the Pest side just north of the Chain Bridge to Margaret Bridge makes for a pleasant stroll, as does the whole of Margaret Island. Boat trips are a good way of viewing the city from another perspective and there are a number of boat operators offering tours from Vigadó tér on the Pest bank.

your boiling frame is a godsend in the heat of summer for cooling off.

4 kids ★★★ **Bathing.** Walk to the Buda side from the fountain and you'll find the Hajós Alfréd Uszoda swimming complex (see p 29), which hosted a recent European Swimming Championship. Further upstream, also facing the Buda side, is the altogether more relaxed holiday camp-like Palatinus (see p 29). For more pampered but indoor thermal bathing head to the Danubuis Health Spa Resort Margitsziget close to Árpád híd. *(6:30am–9:30pm daily. Admission Ft 6,500 (weekdays), Ft 7,700 (weekend).)*

5 kids ★ **Abbey Ruins.** The foundations of the 13th-century St. Margaret's Abbey are located roughly on the middle of the island, Pest side. While there's been some obvious mortaring going on and some modern additions, it is still a nice place to contemplate the past. About another 100m further on, in an upstream direction, there's a replica functioning church. ⏱ *15 min.*

6 ★★ **Watertower.** The watertower stands as a beacon of Hungary's industrial prowess at its time of construction in 1911. Designer and Budapest Engineering University Professor Szilárd Zielinski managed to add a few Art Nouveau touches to the striking 57m/187ft-high structure. The watertower is not currently open but a drink at the theater bar directly underneath is a good way to appreciate it. The bar is the most laidback theater bar I know and one for which flip flops are highly appropriate. ⏱ *10 min.*

7 kids **Japanese Garden.** This cute cranny provides a nice diversion for kids who can spot varied species of fish, turtles, and frogs to the trickling sound of the waterfall. ⏱ *15–30 min.*

8 kids **Musical Well.** The last time I checked this little well out, it was actually talking but hang around until music starts pumping out. ⏱ *15 min.* ●

The watertower dating back to 1911.

Dining Best Bets

Best **Balkan**
★ Kafana Grill Restaurant $–$$
Sörház utca 4 (p 105)

Best **Bistro**
★★ Café Kör $$ *Sas utca 1 (p 99)*

Best **Burger**
★★★ Gresham Kávéház $$$ Four
Seasons Gresham Palace Hotel
Roosevelt tér 5-6 (p 104); ★ Ballet-
cipő *Hajós utca 14 $ (p 103)*

Best **Burrito**
★ Arriba Taqueria $ *Teréz körút 25
(p 103)*

Best **Bargain Gourmet**
★★★ Csalagány 26 $ *Csalogány
utca 26 (p 99)*

Best **Celebrity Chef Meal**
★★★ Matteo $$$ *Pasaréti út 100
(p 102)*

Best **Cheap 'n' Cheerful
Goulash**
★ Pozsonyi kisvendéglő $ *Radnóti
Miklós utca 38 (p 102)*

Best **Chinese**
★★ Momotaro Ramen $$
Széchenyi utca 16 (p 106)

Best **Courtyard Dining**
★★ Fészek $–$$ *Kertész utca 36
(p 99)*

Best **Curry**
★ Indigo $$ *Jókai utca 13 (p 105)*;
★ Taj Mahal $$ *Szondi utca 40 (p 108)*

Best **Danube Dining**
★★ Spoon $$$ *Moored opposite
Hotel Intercontinental (p 107)*

Best **Fin de Siècle Hungarian
Gourmet**
★★★ Vadrózsa $$$$ *Pentelei Mol-
nár utca 5 (p 102)*

Best **Fusion**
★★ Baraka $$$ *Andrássy Hotel
MaMaison Andrássy út 111 (p 103)*

Best **Italian**
★★★ Fausto's Étterem $$$$
Székely Mihály utca 2 (p 104); ★★★
Páva $$$$ *Four Seasons Gresham
Palace Roosevelt tér 5–6*

Best **Pizza**
★★ Il Terzo Cerchio $$ *Dohány
utca 40 (p 104)*; ★★ Trattoria
Toscana $$ *Belgrád rakpart 13
(p 108)*

Best **Retro**
★★★ Kádár $ *Klauzál tér 10 (p 100)*;
★ Menza *Liszt Ferenc tér 2 (p 102)*

Best **Solet (Jewish Bean Stew)**
★★ Fülemüle $$ *Kőfaragó utca 5
(p 99)*

Best **Sushi**
★★ Fuji $$$–$$$$ *Csatárka utca 54
(p 104)*; ★★ Okuyama no Sushi $$$
Kolosy tér 5–6 (p 106)

Best **Wine Restaurant**
★★★ Klassz $$ *Andrássy út 41
(p 101)*

Retro styling at Menza.

Outer Pest Dining

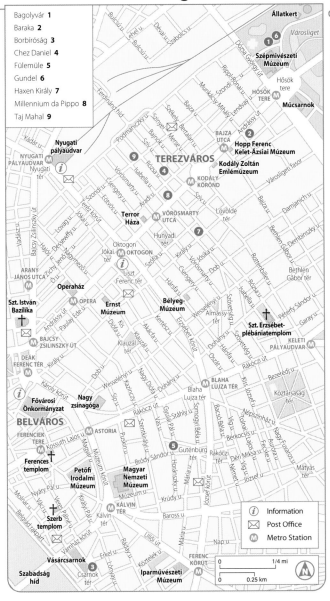

Central Pest Dining

Arigato **1**
Arriba Taqueria **2**
Artesano Spanyol Étterem és Tapas Bár **3**
Balletcipő **4**
Biarritz **5**
Bock Bistro **6**
Café Bouchon **7**
Café Kör **8**
Cyrano **9**
Fausto's Étterem **10**
Fausto's Osteria **11**
Fészek **12**
Firkász **13**
Gerlóczy Kávéház **14**
Goa **15**
Govinda Vegetáriánus Étterem **16**
Gresham Kávéház **17**
Hanna's Kosher Kitchen **18**
Iguana Bar & Grill **19**
Il Terzo Cerchio **20**
Indigo **21**
Kádár Étkezde **22**
Kafana Grill Restaurant **23**
Károlyi Étterem-Káveház **24**
Két Szerecsen Kávéház **25**
Kiskakukk **26**
Kispipa **27**
Klassz **28**
Kőleves **29**
Lou-Lou **30**
M! **31**
Menza **32**
Momotaro Ramen **33**
Mosselen **34**
Oceán Bar & Grill **35**
Okay Italia **36**
Pampas Argentine Steak House **37**
Paris-Budapest Café **38**
Pata Negra **39**
Peppers! Mediterranean Grill **40**
Pozsonyi kisvendéglő **41**
Ristorante Krizia **42**
Segal **43**
Spoon **44**
Tom George Restaurant & Café **45**
Trattoria Toscana **46**

MARGIT HÍD
Margit híd
Újpesti rakpart
Pozsonyi út
Hollán Ernő u.
Tátra u.
Jászai Mari tér
Szt. István körút
Budai alsó rakpart
Duna (Danube)
Pesti alsó rakpart
Balassi Bálint u.
Falk Miksa u.
Honvéd u.
Markó u.
Honvéd tér
Szalay u.
Néprajzi Múzeum
Országház
Kossuth Lajos tér
BATTHYÁNY TÉR
KOSSUTH LAJOS TÉR
Vértanúk tér
Garibaldi u.
Zoltán u.
Szabadság tér
Steindl Imre u.
Nádor u.
Bem rakpart
Széchenyi rakpart
Akadémia u.
Arany János u.
Október 6. u.
Magyar Tudományos Akadémia
Zrínyi u.
Fő út
Roosevelt tér
Mérleg u.
Széchenyi lánchíd
Clark Ádám tér
Eötvös tér
József Attila u.
József nádor tér
Bécsi u.
VÖRÖSMARTY TÉR
Vörösmarty tér
Budavári palota
Vigadó tér
Pesti alsó rakpart
Váralja u.
Attila út
Krisztina körút
Döbrentei u.
Budai alsó rakpart
Petőfi tér
Tabáni plébániatemplom
Belvárosi plébániatemplom
Kereszt u.
Március 15. tér
Rác gyógyfürdő
Erzsébet híd
Döbrentei tér
Szt. Gellért emlékmű
Rudas gyógyfürdő
Orom u.
Szt. Gellért rakpart
GELLÉRTHEGY
Citadella

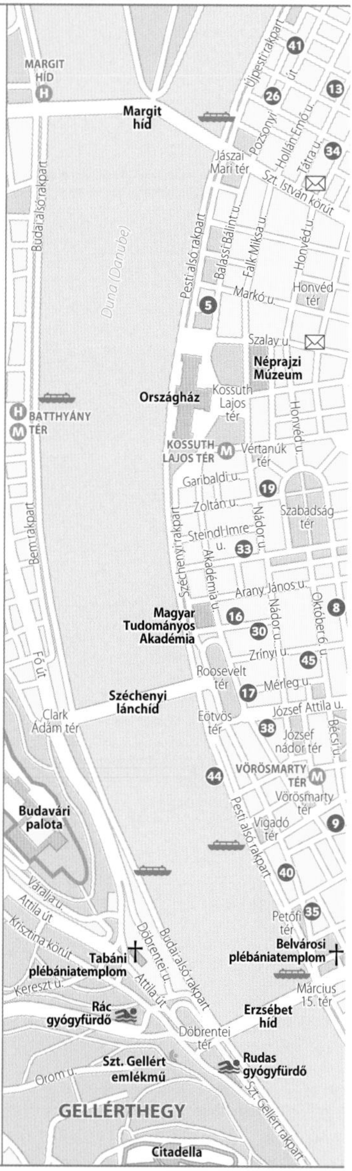

Information
Post Office
Metro Station
HÉV Station
Boat Pier

Buda Dining

Legend:

- (i) Information
- ⊠ Post Office
- Ⓜ Metro Station
- Ⓗ HÉV Station
- 🚢 Boat Pier

```
0          1/2 mi
0      0.5 km
```

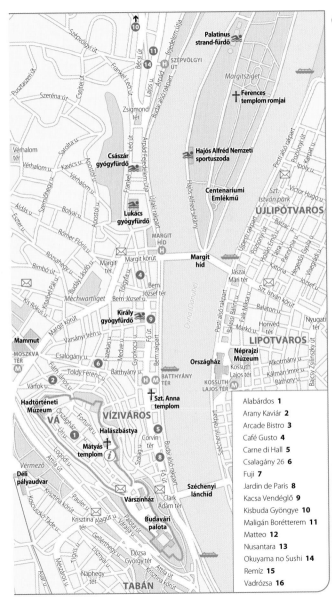

Alabárdos **1**

Arany Kaviár **2**

Arcade Bistro **3**

Café Gusto **4**

Carne di Hall **5**

Csalagány 26 **6**

Fuji **7**

Jardin de Paris **8**

Kacsa Vendéglő **9**

Kisbuda Gyöngye **10**

Maligán Borétterem **11**

Matteo **12**

Nusantara **13**

Okuyama no Sushi **14**

Remíz **15**

Vadrózsa **16**

Budapest Dining A to Z

Hungarian

★★ **Alabárdos** BUDA *HUNGARIAN* Gourmet heaven in a Gothic setting with unique takes on Hungarian cuisine from only the best in local fresh ingredients. *Országház utca 2.* ☎ *1/356-0851. Entrees Ft 3,300–Ft 6,500. AE, MC, V. Dinner Mon–Fri. Lunch & dinner Sat. Bus: 16/16A1/116 to Szentháromság tér. Map p 96.*

★★ **Arcade Bistro** BUDA *HUNGARIAN/CONTINENTAL* Stylishly modern sister of Pest's Café Kör (see p 99), ups the gourmet stakes with delicacies like Mangalica pork with dried tomato risotto. *Kiss János Altábornagy utca 38.* ☎ *1/225-1696. Entrees Ft 2,490–Ft 4,470. MC, V. Lunch & dinner Mon–Sat. Tram: 59/61 to Csörsz utca. Map p 96.*

Bagolyvár OUTER PEST *HUNGARIAN* Run by some 20 women, the 'Owl's Castle' does Magyar cuisine, in an early 20th-century setting, as a Hungarian mom makes it. This sister of gourmet Gundel (p 100) is housed in a mock Transylvanian castle. *Állatkerti út 2.* ☎ *1/468-3110.*

Classic Hungarian served up at Biarritz.

Ft 1,500–Ft 4,000. AE, DC, MC, V. Lunch & dinner daily. Metro: M1 to Hősök tere. Map p 93.

Biarritz CENTRAL PEST *HUNGARIAN/INTERNATIONAL* A few steps away from Parliament, this stylish eatery does classic Hungarian and continental dishes well, but excels in merging the two. Nice summer terrace. *Kossuth Lajos tér 18 (entrance on Balassi Bálint utca).* ☎ *1/311-4413. Entrees Ft 2,950–Ft 5,450. AE, MC, V. Lunch & dinner daily. Tram: 2 to Szalay utca. Map p 94.*

★ **Bock Bistro** CENTRAL PEST *HUNGARIAN/MEDITERRANEAN* Luxury Latin look with tasty tapas and succulent meat, doubling as a shop for Villány producer József Bock's wines. *Corinthia Grand Hotel Royal, Erzsébet körút 43–49.* ☎ *1/321-0340. Entrees Ft 3,100–Ft 5,100. MC, V. Lunch & dinner Mon–Sat. Metro: M1 to Oktogon; tram: 4/6 to Oktogon. Map p 94.*

Borbíróság OUTER PEST *HUNGARIAN* With 60 wines available by the glass, the 'Court of Wines' is ideal for sampling local wines alongside quality fusion-free Hungarian dishes. *Csarnok tér 5.* ☎ *1/219-0902. Entrees Ft 2,250–Ft 4,250. AE, MC, V. Lunch & dinner Mon–Sat. Metro: M3 to Kálvin tér. Tram: 47/49 to Kálvin tér. Map p 93.*

★ **Café Bouchon** CENTRAL PEST *HUNGARIAN/FRENCH* Welcoming bistro with Art Nouveau influences in the décor and new takes on Hungarian cuisine and continental favorites. *Zichy Jenő utca 33.* ☎ *1/353-4094. Entrees Ft 2,100–Ft 4,690. No credit cards. Lunch & dinner Mon–Sat. Metro: M1 to Oktogon, M3 to Nyugati pu. Map p 94.*

Try Villány producer József Bock's wine at the Bock Bistro.

★★ **Café Kör** CENTRAL PEST *HUNGARIAN/CONTINENTAL* Buzzing bistro and although it's a bit cramped, plenty of bums on seats ensures ever-consistent Hungarian and continental fare. *Sas utca 17.* ☎ *1/311-0053. Entrees Ft 1,870–Ft 4,190. No credit cards. Lunch & dinner Mon–Sat. Metro: M3 to Arany János utca. Map p 94.*

★★★ **Csalagány 26** BUDA *HUNGARIAN/CONTINENTAL* Remarkable value lunch menu makes this plain-looking bistro a good bet, although it's more expensive in the evening. Dishes are prepared using only fresh seasonal ingredients.

Café Kör.

Csalogány utca 26. ☎ *1/201-7892. Entrees Ft 1,400–Ft 4,000. MC, V. Lunch & dinner Tues–Fri, dinner only Sat; closed 20 Jul–5 Aug. Metro: M2 to Batthyány tér. Map p 96.*

★★ kids **Fészek** CENTRAL PEST *HUNGARIAN* This artists' club, with its cloistered courtyard, is steeped in atmosphere. Excellent sztrapacska (flour and potato dumplings with bacon and ewe cheese). *Kertész utca 36.* ☎ *1/322-6043. Entrees Ft 1,500–Ft 2,300. No credit cards. Lunch & dinner daily. Tram: 4/6 to Király utca. Map p 94.*

★ **Firkász** CENTRAL PEST *HUNGARIAN* Fine cuts are prepared from refined recipes at Firkász. Old newspaper articles are pasted to the walls and a piano player enhances the old-world atmosphere in the evening. *Tátra utca 18.* ☎ *1/450-1119. Entrees Ft 1,490–Ft 4,900. MC, V. Lunch & dinner daily. Tram: 2/4/6 to Jászai Mari tér. Map p 94.*

★★ **Fülemüle** OUTER PEST *HUNGARIAN/JEWISH* 'The Nightingale' serves a non-kosher blend of Hungarian and Jewish cuisine that predates modern fusion trends in a warm family setting. *Kőfaragó utca 5.* ☎ *1/266-7947. Entrees Ft 1,900–Ft 4,700. MC, V. Lunch & dinner daily. Metro: M2 to Blaha Lujza tér. Tram: 4/6 to Blaha Lujza tér. Map p 93.*

★★★ Gerlóczy Kávéház

CENTRAL PEST *HUNGARIAN CONTINENTAL* Lovely Parisian-style café serving homemade pastry for breakfast and creative lunch and dinner offerings with some nice twists. *Gerlóczy utca 1.* ☎ *1/235-0953. Entrees Ft 1,890–Ft 3,900. AE, MC, V. Breakfast, lunch & dinner daily. Metro: M1/M2/M3 to Deák tér. Map p 94.*

★★ Gundel OUTER PEST *HUNGARIAN*

A feast of the finest china, tablecloths, artworks, and splendor entice you before you even get to the food. Gundel has been moving into the present serving Hungarian cuisine in a lighter but still expressive way via better use of seasonal ingredients. If you don't feel like dressing up, Gundel's 1894 Wine Cellar is more subterranean. *Állatkerti út 2.* ☎ *1/468-4040. Entrees Ft 3,900–Ft 10,620. AE, DC, MC, V. Lunch & dinner daily. Metro: M1 to Hősök tere. Map p 93.*

Hanna's Kosher Kitchen CENTRAL PEST *HUNGARIAN KOSHER*

Hungarian classics, like the simple but crispy and succulent Kosher chicken fried in breadcrumbs, are served in this atmospheric, no-frills 1970s-style dining room. Roast duck, beef goulash, and stuffed cabbage also feature. *Dob utca 35.* ☎ *1/342-1072. Entrees Ft 1,500–Ft 1,800. AE, MC, V. Lunch & dinner daily. Map p 94.*

★★ Haxen Király OUTER PEST *HUNGARIAN/BAVARIAN*

Pine-paneling and wooden furnishings galore welcome carnivores with generous portions of quality goose liver, goose leg, wild boar, and pork knuckle. *Király utca 100.* ☎ *1/351-6793. Entrees Ft 2,500–Ft 3,500. AE, MC, V. Lunch & dinner daily. Metro: M1/M2/M3 to Deák tér. Map p 93.*

★ Kacsa Vendéglő BUDA *HUNGARIAN*

Hungary is known for its delectable duck, old-fashioned hospitality and, once upon a time, for quality service. You get all this and more at 'Duck'. *Fő utca 75.* ☎ *1/201-9992. Entrees Ft 3,600–Ft 5,600. AE, MC, V. Lunch & dinner daily. Metro: M2 to Battyhány tér. Map p 96.*

★★★ Kádár Étkezde CENTRAL PEST *HUNGARIAN/JEWISH*

Non-Kosher, Jewish-like crispy goose leg with red cabbage served in a real retro setting where guests often share tables. The solet bean stew and matzo ball soup are on the menu Saturdays only. *Klauzál tér 10.*

Old world charm at Firkász.

include goose liver cream soup. *Pozsonyi út 12.* ☎ *1/450-0829. Entrees Ft 2,000–Ft 3,000. AE, MC, V. Lunch & dinner daily. Tram: 2/4/6 to Jászai Mari tér. Map p 94.*

★ **Kispipa** CENTRAL PEST *HUNGARIAN* Traditional Hungarian and old-world continental dishes with lots of game on the menu. Expect a refined pre-war vibe and enjoy the piano player after 7pm. *Akácfa utca 38.* ☎ *1/342-2587 or 1/342-3969. Entrees Ft 980–Ft 5,560. AE, DC, MC, V. Lunch & dinner daily. Metro: M1 to Oktogon. Tram: 4/6 to Wesselényi utca. Map p 94.*

★★★ **Klassz** CENTRAL PEST *HUNGARIAN/CONTINENTAL* Foie gras risottos, lamb knuckle, and Mangalica pig steak feature at this creative and hip minimalist-designed wine restaurant. No bookings so turn up early. *Andrássy út 41. No phone. Entrees Ft 1,490–Ft 2,890. AE, MC, V. Lunch & dinner Mon–Sat; lunch only Sun. Metro: M1 to Opera. Map p 94.*

★★ **Kőleves** CENTRAL PEST *HUNGARIAN* Hearty Hungarian meat dishes plus Jewish, international, and veggie options are available here at

Seasonal Hungarian dishes at Gundel.

☎ *1/321-3622. Entrees Ft 750–Ft 1,800. No credit cards. Lunch Tues–Sat. Tram: 4/6 to Király utca. Map p 94.*

★ **Károlyi Étterem-Kávéház** CENTRAL PEST *HUNGARIAN/MEDITERRANEAN* Good value restaurant-cum-coffee house in the grand Károlyi Palace featuring a restored Biedermeier interior and a sublime courtyard. *Károlyi Mihály utca 16.* ☎ *1/328-0240. Entrees Ft 1,250–Ft 3,250. AE, MC, V. Lunch & dinner daily. Metro: M3 to Ferenciek-tere or Kálvin tér. Map p 94.*

★★★ **Kisbuda Gyöngye** BUDA *HUNGARIAN* High-end Hungarian with continental and Mediterranean twists like goose liver risotto served in a charming early 20th-century setting that's well worth the trek out to Óbuda. *Kenyeres u. 34.* ☎ *1/368-9227. Entrees Ft 1,800–Ft 4,200. AE, MC, V. Lunch & dinner Mon–Sat. Tram: 17 to Nagyszombat utca. Map p 96.*

★★ **Kiskakukk** CENTRAL PEST *HUNGARIAN/CONTINENTAL* Arches and heavy wood depict the original 'Little Cuckoo' restaurant, which dates back to 1913. Delicacies

Vegetarian options available at the hip Kőleves.

Magyar recipes and a top wine list at Maligán Borétterem.

the cool and slightly alternative 'Stone soup'. *Kazinczy utca 35/Dob utca 26 corner.* ☎ *1/322-1011. Entrees Ft 1,280–Ft 3,680. AE, MC, V. Lunch & dinner daily. Metro: M1/M2/M3 to Deák tér. Map p 94.*

★ **Maligán Borétterem** BUDA *HUNGARIAN* This classy cellar eatery is one of a number of 'wine restaurants' but this one also comes up with the culinary goods via creative and subtle new-style Magyar recipes. Real gems among the extensive wine list, and tasting measures also served. *Lajos utca 38.* ☎ *1/240-9010. Entrees Ft 2,900–Ft 3,900. AE, DC, MC, V. Lunch & dinner Tues–Sat Bus: 86/160/260 to Kolosy tér. Map p 96.*

★★★ **kids Matteo** BUDA *HUNGARIAN* Subtle but expressive flavors in a Bauhaus setting from TV chef Péter Buday who mixes with diners as he works out which Magyar Med concoction they might like. *Pasaréti út 100.* ☎ *1/392-7531. Entrees Ft 1,600–Ft 5,900. MC, V. Lunch & dinner daily. Tram: 56 to Pasaréti tér (last stop). Map p 96.*

★ **Menza** CENTRAL PEST *HUNGARIAN* Popular spot for unpretentious Hungarian fare on fashionable Liszt Ferenc tér. The fun retro kitsch décor is based on the ubiquitous Socialist-era canteen. *Liszt Ferenc tér 2.* ☎ *1/413-1482. Entrees Ft 1,490–Ft 3,490. AE, MC, V. Lunch & dinner daily. Metro: M1 to Oktogon. Tram: 4/6 to Oktogon. Map p 94.*

★ **Pozsonyi kisvendéglő** CENTRAL PEST *HUNGARIAN* People queue up patiently for reassuringly old-fashioned, cheap, and cheerful Hungarian classics. Grab a beer as you wait or nip in early. *Radnóti Miklós utca 38 (corner of Pozsonyi út).* ☎ *1/329-2911. Entrees Ft 800–Ft 1,900. No credit cards. Tram: 2/4/6 to Jászai Mari tér. Map p 94.*

★★★ **Vadrózsa** BUDA *HUNGARIAN* Fine dining turn-of-the-century style, in a Baroque villa circled by a plush garden. Goose liver, gorgeous-looking cuts of meat, game, and fish will be paraded enticingly before you. *Pentelei Molnár utca 15.* ☎ *1/326-5817. Entrees Ft 4,400–Ft 5,980. AE, DC, MC, V. Lunch & dinner daily. Bus: 11/91 to Vend utca. Map p 96.*

International Cuisines

★ **Arany Kaviár** BUDA *RUSSIAN* The best in Beluga, Sevruga, and Iranian caviar, blinis and pickled fish, plus posh Stroganoff in a retro Romanov setting. *Ostrom utca 19.* ☎ *1/201-6737 or 1/225-7370. Entrees Ft 3,500–Ft 9,500. AE, DC, MC, V. Lunch & dinner daily. Metro: M2 to Moszkva tér. Tram: 4/6 to Moszkva tér. Map p 96.*

★ **Arigato** CENTRAL PEST *JAPANESE* This threadbare Japanese-run joint is popular for the highly authentic, regularly changing and healthy-looking meat, rice, noodle, and veg combos, plus sushi. *Ó utca 3.* ☎ *1/353-3549. Ft 1,850–Ft 5,000. AE, DC, MC, V. Lunch & dinner*

Mon–Sat. Metro: M3 to Arany János utca. Map p 94.

★ **Arriba Taqueria** CENTRAL PEST *MEXICAN* Freshly steamed tacos, quesadillas, and burritos with juicy steak, chorizo, carnitas, and fresh condiments galore. Colorful murals. *Teréz körút 25.* ☎ *1/374-0057. Entrees Ft 1,200–Ft 1,600. AE, DC, MC, V. Lunch & dinner Mon–Sat. Metro: M1 to Oktogon. Tram: 4/6 to Oktogon. Map p 94.*

★★ **Artesano Spanyol Étterem és Tapas Bár** CENTRAL PEST *SPANISH* Refined Spanish regional dishes and fine tapas in a fashionable setting straight from 'new Spain'. Cheap lunch menu on weekdays. *Ó utca 24–26.* ☎ *1/688-1696. Entrees Ft 1,800–Ft 3,200. MC, V. Lunch & dinner Mon–Sat. Metro: M1 to Oktogon. Map p 94.*

★ **Balletcipő** CENTRAL PEST *INTERNATIONAL* This gastro pub's eclectic menu somehow works, especially the Philly Cheese Steak sandwich. Spills out onto a shabby chic pedestrian street in summer. *Hajós utca 14 (corner of Ó utca).* ☎ *1/269-3114. Entrees Ft 1,580–Ft 2,950. No credit cards. Lunch & dinner daily. Metro: M1 to Opera or M3 to Arany János utca. Map p 94.*

★★★ **Baraka** OUTER PEST *FUSION* Dark, sleek and minimalist, Baraka fits well into the Bauhaus Andrássy Hotel (see p 140) and sets the fusion standards with ambitious-sounding but delicious concoctions. *MaMaison Andrássy Hotel. Andrássy út 111.* ☎ *1/483-1355. Entrees Ft 2,900–Ft 6,900. AE, DC, MC, V. Lunch & dinner daily. Metro: M1 to Bajza utca. Map p 93.*

Café Gusto BUDA *ITALIAN* Exquisite Italianate salads and starters, cold pastas, and sumptuous Tiramisu served in an intimate, antique-laden, bijou setting. *Frankel Leó u. 12.* ☎ *1/316-3970. Entrees Ft 1,000–Ft 2,000. Breakfast, lunch & dinner daily. Metro: M2 to Battyhány tér. Tram: 4/6 to Margit hid Budai hídfő. Map p 96.*

Carne di Hall BUDA *BELGIAN/ INTERNATIONAL* Croquette de crevettes, from fresh juicy shrimps, and melt-in-the-mouth steak tartare feature at this attractive Buda waterfront eatery. *Bem rakpart 20.* ☎ *1/201-8137. Entrees Ft 3,000– Ft 5,000. AE, MC, V. Lunch & dinner daily. Metro: M2 to Battyhány tér. Map p 96.*

Chez Daniel OUTER PEST *FRENCH* Walk out if the owner-chef is asleep on the bar, but when he's on song this is nouveau French cuisine par-excellence. Lovely courtyard in summer. *Sziv utca 32.* ☎ *1/302-4039. Entrees Ft 2,000–Ft 5,000. AE, DC, MC, V. Lunch & dinner daily. Metro: M1 to Kodály körönd. Map p 93.*

★ **Cyrano** CENTRAL PEST *INTER-NATIONAL* Pricey but consistently creative restaurant offering new fresh-ingredient fuelled takes on old

Mexican fare at Arriba Taqueria.

Try Fuji for great sushi lunch boxes.

favorites. *Kristóf tér 7–8.* ☎ *1/226-3096. Entrees Ft 3,690–4790. AE, MC, V. Breakfast, lunch & dinner daily. Metro: M1/M2/M3 to Deák tér. Map p 94.*

★★★ **Fausto's Étterem** CENTRAL PEST *ITALIAN* Exquisite Italian traditional cuisine enhanced by subtle wider-world touches and flawless ingredients. Classy minimalist décor. *Székely Mihály utca 2.* ☎ *1/877-6210. Entrees Ft 2,200–Ft 6,000. AE, MC, V. Lunch & dinner Mon–Fri; dinner only Sat. Metro: M1 to Opera. Map p 94.*

★★★ **Fausto's Osteria** CENTRAL PEST *ITALIAN* Fausto's traditional take on Italian cuisine is informal but gets the ingredients just right. Like its sibling Fausto's Etterem, it also received a recommended tag from Michelin in 2007. *Dohány utca 5.* ☎ *1/269-6806. Entrees Ft 1,850–Ft 4,600. AE, MC, V. Lunch & dinner Mon–Sat. Metro: M2 to Astoria. Map p 94.*

★★ **Fuji** kids BUDA *JAPANESE* Sushi is rolled before watchful customers in a highly authentic setting. Great lunch boxes include sashimi, tempura, and grilled fish. *Csatárka utca 54 (corner of Zöldlomb utca & Zödkert utca).* ☎ *1/325-7111. Entrees Ft 3,500–Ft 9,800. AE, DC, MC, V. Lunch & dinner daily. Bus: 29 to Zöldkert út. Map p 96.*

Goa CENTRAL PEST *ASIAN INTERNATIONAL* The chichi generic Asian décor works as a backdrop to the refined pan-Asian specialties, including sushi, plus pasta dishes, excellent salads, and ciabatta sandwiches. *Andrássy út 8.* ☎ *1/302-2570. Entrees Ft 1,500–Ft 2,500. AE, MC, V. Lunch & dinner daily. Metro: M1 to Bajcsy-Zsilinszky út. Map p 94.*

Govinda Vegetáriánus Étterem CENTRAL PEST *INDIAN* Great value vegetarian Indian food from the Krishnas in this funky cellar. Wash it all down with the spicy homemade soft drinks. *Vigyázó Ferenc utca 4.* ☎ *1/269-1625. Entrees Ft 1,550–Ft 1,850 (menus). No credit cards. Lunch & dinner Mon–Sat. Metro: M3 to Arany János utca. Map p 94.*

★★★ **Gresham Kávéház** CENTRAL PEST *CONTINENTAL/ GOURMET ITALIAN* At Gresham you'll find fine continental and now also Hungarian cuisine with sublime international touches and a view to the Chain Bridge. A suave coffee house-cum-bistro inside an Art Nouveau landmark. *Four Seasons Gresham Palace Hotel, Roosvevelt tér 5–6.* ☎ *1/268-5100. Entrees Ft 3,600–Ft 5,800. AE, DC, MC, V. Lunch & dinner daily. Metro: M1 to Vörösmarty tér. Tram: 2 to Roosevelt tér. Map p 94.*

★★ **Il Terzo Cerchio** CENTRAL PEST *ITALIAN* A strong Italian contingent frequents this upmarket trattoria whose house pizza is a tasty assortment of tomato, buffalo mozzarella, Parma ham, and ruccola (arugula/rocket). *Dohány utca 40.* ☎ *1/354-0788. Entrees Ft 1,550–Ft 5,500. MC, V. Lunch & dinner daily. Metro: M2 to Blaha Lujza tér. Map p 94.*

Iguana Bar & Grill CENTRAL PEST *TEX-MEX* The American expat crowd pile in for Tex-Mex that approaches the quality from back home. Enjoy the potent margaritas and a guaranteed lively Cantina atmosphere. *Zoltán utca 16.* ☎ *1/301-0215. Entrees Ft 1,890–Ft 3,990. AE, DC, MC, V. Lunch & dinner daily. Metro: M2 to Kossuth tér. Map p 94.*

★ **Indigo** CENTRAL PEST *INDIAN* A fine Indian all-rounder with an impressive range of classic Indian dishes, but particularly excelling in lamb curries. The comfy chic décor makes this a place to linger. *Jókai utca 13.* ☎ *1/428-2187. Entrees Ft 2,000–Ft 3,000. Lunch & dinner daily. Metro: M1 to Oktogon. Tram: 4/6 to Oktogon. Map p 94.*

★★ **Jardin de Paris** BUDA *FRENCH* Authentic foie gras, lamb, and hanger (onglet) steak can be savored in this beautiful Baroque house. In the summer months it's lovely to dine in the garden. Ask for the excellent complimentary shredded duck pâté rillettes should it fail to arrive. *Fő utca 20.* ☎ *1/201-0047. Entrees Ft 1,500–Ft 5,200. AE, DC, MC, V. Lunch & dinner daily. Metro: M2 to Batthyány tér. Map p 96.*

★ **Kafana Grill Restaurant** CENTRAL PEST *SERBIAN/ INTERNATIONAL* The cool rustic décor with funky urban paintings is the perfect setting to enjoy succulent Serbian ground meat specialties ćevapčići and pljeskavica. Also a

pub. *Sörház utca 4.* ☎ *1/266-2274. Entrees Ft 1,400– Ft 3,900. No credit cards. Dinner daily. Metro: M3 to Ferenciek tere. Tram: 2 to Fővám tér. Map p 94.*

★★ **Két Szerecsen Kávéház** CENTRAL PEST *MEDITERRANEAN* Med-influenced cuisine and décor, with subtle Magyar and international touches. The 'Two Saracens' is also good for tapas or just a drink. Nice terrace. *Nagymező utca 14.* ☎ *1/343-1984. Entrees Ft 2,160–Ft 3,990. DC, MC, V. Lunch & dinner daily. Metro: M1 to Opera. Map p 94.*

★★★ **Lou-Lou** CENTRAL PEST *INTERNATIONAL* Lovely and consistent creative fusion of Hungarian and French cuisine, with subtle touches coming from further afield. Sleek décor. *Vigyázó Ferenc utca 4.* ☎ *1/312-4505. Entrees Ft 4,400–Ft 10,900. AE, V, MC, AE. Lunch & dinner Mon–Fri, dinner only Sat. Metro: M2 to Kossuth Lajos tér. Map p 94.*

★ **M!** CENTRAL PEST *FRENCH/ HUNGARIAN* No-nonsense bijou bistro that lets the creative and daily changing menu do the talking. Well worth visiting again now that Francophile founder Miklós Sulyok is

Lou Lou offers a fusion of Hungarian and French cuisine.

back. *Kertész utca 48.* ☎ *1/342-8991. Entrees Ft 1,400–Ft 2,800. No credit cards. Dinner daily. Metro: M1 to Oktogon. Tram: 4/6 to Király utca. Map p 94.*

Millennium da Pippo OUTER
PEST *ITALIAN* Resembling a station of the Millennium Underground that zips under the same street, the food is reassuringly rustic and good quality. *Andrássy út 76 (corner of Rózsa utca).* ☎ *1/374-0880. Entrees Ft 1,300–Ft 4,050. MC, V. Lunch & dinner daily. Metro: M1 to Vörösmárty utca. Map p 93.*

★★ Momotaro Ramen CENTRAL
PEST *ASIAN* The excellent ramen noodle soup washed down by the free tea may suffice, but tasty Szechuan mains delight. *Széchenyi utca 16.* ☎ *1/269-3802. Entrees under Ft 800. No credit cards. Lunch & dinner daily. Metro: M2 to Kossuth tér. Tram: 2 to Kossuth tér. Map p 94.*

Mosselen CENTRAL PEST *BELGIAN/ CONTINENTAL* The imagination behind the names of dishes like 'The Favorite of the Leuven Professors' (duck steak) also goes into the creative Belgian-influenced fare. Eight Belgian beers on draft. *Pannónia utca 14 (corner of Katona József utca).* ☎ *1/452-0535. Entrees Ft 1,800–Ft 4,890. AE, V, MC. Lunch & dinner daily. Tram: 2/4/6 to Jászai Mari tér. Map p 94.*

Nusantara BUDA *INDONESIAN*
Fine attention to detail both in terms of the high-quality Indonesian from native chefs featuring regional specialties starting with Lumpia (Javan spring rolls) and the sleek softly lit décor. *Városmajor utca 88.* ☎ *1/201-1478. Entrees Ft 2,390–Ft 3,790. MC, V. Lunch & dinner daily. Tram: 56 to Szent János Kórház. Map p 96.*

★★ Oceán Bar & Grill CENTRAL
PEST *SEAFOOD* Creative cooking is on the menu here, but I prefer to ask what's fresh in and have it grilled. Nautical touches and the mighty Danube outside are conducive for an ocean feast. The adjoining Deli does take-out fish 'n' chips. *Petőfi tér 3.* ☎ *1/266-1826. Entrees Ft 2,300–Ft 9,750. AE, MC, V. Lunch & dinner daily. Metro: M1 to Vörösmarty tér. Tram: 2 to Vigadó tér. Map p 94.*

Okay Italia CENTRAL PEST
ITALIAN This Pest trattoria packs them in with well-priced classics and mini-skirted waitresses. If it's full, its identically named twin is nearby at Nyugati tér 6. *Szent István körút 20.* ☎ *1/349-229. Entrees Ft 1,450–Ft 3,650. DC, MC, V. Lunch & dinner daily. Metro: M3 to Nyugatipu. Tram: 2/4/6 to Jászai Mari tér. Map p 94.*

★★ Okuyama no Sushi BUDA
JAPANESE Stellar sushi is rolled from ocean delights by the intricate Japanese hand of Tokyo-trained chef Sachi Okuyama in this no-nonsense cellar joint. Cooked options, too. *Kolosy tér 5–6.* ☎ *1/250-8256. Entrees Ft 1,200–Ft 5,000. No credit cards. Lunch & dinner Tues–Sun. Bus: 6/60/86 to Kolosy tér.*

★ Pampas Argentine Steak
House CENTRAL PEST *STEAK* Stylish blood red décor and juicy steaks from quality imported Argentine Angus cuts, T-bone from the UK, plus Japanese Kobe. *Vámház körút 6.* ☎ *1/411-1750. Entrees Ft 2,600–Ft 14,900. MC, V. Lunch & dinner daily. Metro: M3 to Kálvin tér. Tram: 47/49 to Kálvin tér. Map p 94.*

★★ kids Paris-Budapest Café
CENTRAL PEST *FRENCH/HUNGARIAN* Enjoyable nouvelle French cuisine, plus a lighter, refreshing take on Hungarian staples. It's sleek with an open kitchen and views to the Chain Bridge. *Sofitel Budapest; Roosevelt tér 2.* ☎ *1/235-5600. Entrees Ft 4,000–Ft 6,600. AE, DC, MC, V.*

Lunch & dinner daily. Metro: M1 to Kossuth tér. Tram: 2 to Roosevelt tér. Map p 94.

Pata Negra CENTRAL PEST *SPANISH* Traditional, tasty tapas with many of the ingredients like jamon and manchego sheep's cheese imported from Spain. Almost authentic tiled interior plus seats outside next to a church. *Kálvin tér 8.* ☎ *1/215-5616. Entrees Ft 850–Ft 2,200. No credit cards. Lunch & dinner daily. Metro: M3 to Kálvin. Map p 94.*

★★ kids Peppers! Mediterranean Grill CENTRAL PEST *MEDITERRANEAN* Delicious Mediterranean-style dishes from local ingredients plus imported salumi to be enjoyed in a stylish setting. *Budapest Marriott Hotel; Apáczai Csere János utca 4.* ☎ *1/737-7377. Entrees Ft 1,400–Ft 5,900. AC, DC, MC, V. Lunch & dinner Mon–Sat. Metro: M1 to Vörösmarty tér. Map p 94.*

★★ Remiz BUDA *HUNGARIAN/ CONTINENTAL* Remíz has a classy casual atmosphere. The front room features a raised alcove that resembles the front of a tram. In summer,

tasty spare ribs are grilled up in the lovely garden. ☎ *1/275-1396. Entrees Ft 1,500–Ft 3,000. Budakeszi út 5. AE, MC, V. Lunch & dinner daily. Tram: 17. Bus: 22 to Szépilona. Map p 96.*

★★ Ristorante Krizia CENTRAL PEST *ITALIAN* A charming and hardly discovered slice of Italy where a savvy touch is applied to traditional Italian cuisine, making poor man's food a rich experience. *Mozsár utca 12.* ☎ *1/331-8711. Entrees Ft 2,680–Ft 8,500. AE, MC, V. Lunch & dinner Mon–Sat. Metro: M1 to Oktogon. Tram: 4/6 to Oktogon. Map p 94.*

★ Segal CENTRAL PEST *FUSION* Fab fusion from the chef of the original Baraka (p 103), who is now in his own place showing daring simplicity and a philosophy of which ingredients to combine, and which not. *Óutca 43-49.* ☎ *1/328-0774. Entrees Ft 3,200–Ft 5,500. AE, DC, MC, V. Dinner only Mon–Sat. Metro: M2 to Astoria. Map p 94.*

★★ Spoon DANUBE PEST SIDE *INTERNATIONAL* Spoon is the pick of the flotilla of boat restaurants,

Fab fusion at Segal.

although the classy cuisine itself warrants a visit regardless of the inspiring Buda views and cool decor. Ocean fresh fish and seafood, and quality meat feature strongly. *Opposite Hotel Intercontinental.* ☎ *1/411-0933. AE, DC, MC, V. Lunch & dinner. Metro: M1 to Vörösmarty tér. Map p 94.*

★ **Taj Mahal** OUTER PEST *INDIAN* Highly consistent traditional and authentic curry house specializing in Karahi, Balti, Handi, and Tandoori dishes. Cricket games are screened. *Szondi utca 40.* ☎ *1/301-0447. Entrees Ft 1,000–Ft 3,000. AE, MC, V. Lunch & dinner Tues–Sun. Metro: M1 to Nyugati pu. Tram: 4/6 to Nyugati pu. Map p 93.*

Tom George Restaurant & Café CENTRAL PEST *HUNGARIAN/ INTERNATIONAL* A trendy but reliably creative gourmet menu consisting of Hungarian, continental, Asian (including Thai curries), and sushi, all to a high level. *Október 6. utca 8.* ☎ *1/266-3525. Entrees Ft 2,800–Ft 7,900. AE, DC, MC, V. Lunch & dinner daily. Metro: M1/M2/M3 to Deák tér. Map p 94.*

★★ **Trattoria Toscana** CENTRAL PEST *ITALIAN* Refined Tuscan

Spoon.

cuisine to be relished in this rustic restaurant with authentic wooden beams and red bricks. Fabulous carpaccio (marinated raw beef), fresh pasta, brick oven-baked pizzas, seafood galore, and tasty T-bone are among my favorites. In summer enjoy the tranquil river view from the terrace. *Belgrád rakpart 13.* ☎ *1/327-0045. Entrees Ft 2,390– Ft 5,250. AE, MC, V. Lunch & dinner daily. Tram: 2 to Március 15. tér. Map p 94.* ●

Trattoria Toscana.

7 The Best **Nightlife**

Nightlife Best Bets

Best Al Fresco Bar
★★★ Holdudvar, *Margaret Island*
(p 123)

Best Boho Bar
★★ Kiadó Kocsma, *Jókai tér 3*
(p 118) and ★★★ Sark, *Klauzál tér*
14 (p 120)

Best Comic Strip Décor
★★ Szóda, *Wesselényi utca 18*
(p 120)

Best Courtyard Bar
★★★ Mumus, *Dob utca 18 (p 123)*

Best Dive Bar
Mátravidéki Borozó, *Corvin tér 1*
(p 121)

Best Garage Bar
★★ Kuplung, *Király utca 46 (p 118)*

Best Gay Club
★★★ CoXx Men's, *Dohány utca 38*
(p 124)

Alfresco drinking at Holdudvar.

Best Glitzy Dance Club
★★★ Dokk, *Hajógyárisziget 122*
(p 124)

Best Intimate Night Club
★★★ Fészek Club, *Kertész utca 36*
(p 124) and ★★★ Piaf, *Nagymező*
utca 25 (p 124)

Best Lesbian Hospitality
★★ Café Eklektika, *Nagymező utca*
30 (p 124)

Best Martini
★★★ Gresham Bar, *Four Seasons*
Gresham Palace Hotel, Roosevelt tér
5–6 (p 117)

Best Place to Drink with the
Locals
★ Wichmann, *Kazinczy utca 55*
(p 120)

Best Place to Show off under
the Stars
★★★ Bed Beach, *Hajógyárisziget*
(p 121)

Best Place to Watch English
Premier League Soccer
★★ Caledonian Scottish Pub,
Mozsár utca 9 (p 116)

Best Retro Bar
★★ Bambi Presszó, *Frankel Leó*
utca 2–4 (p 116)

Best Rooftop Terrace
★★★ Corvintető, *Corvin Áruház,*
Blaha Lujza tér 1–2 (p 122)

Best Something for Everyone
Nightspot
★★ Club Inside/Buddha
Beach/Retro Beach, *Közraktár utca*
9–11 (p 124)

Best Thirty-something Boho
Hangout
★★★ Ellátó, *Klauzál tér 2 (p 117)*

Buda Nightlife

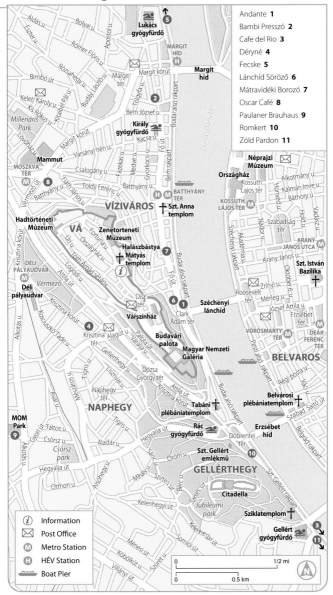

Andante **1**
Bambi Presszó **2**
Cafe del Rio **3**
Déryné **4**
Fecske **5**
Lánchíd Söröző **6**
Mátravidéki Borozó **7**
Oscar Café **8**
Paulaner Brauhaus **9**
Romkert **10**
Zöld Pardon **11**

(i) Information
⊠ Post Office
Ⓜ Metro Station
Ⓗ HÉV Station
⚓ Boat Pier

0		1/2 mi
0	0.5 km	

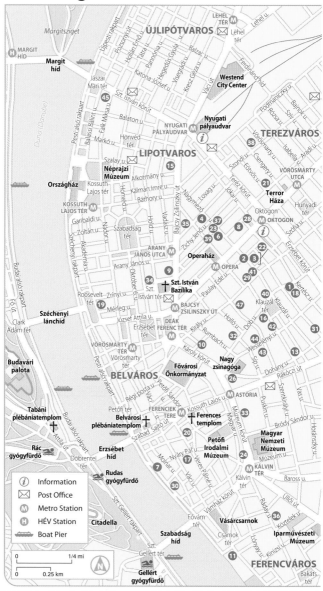

Margitsziget

MARGIT HÍD

Margit híd

ÚJLIPÓTVÁROS

LEHEL TÉR

Lehel tér

Westend City Center

Nyugati pályaudvar

NYUGATI PÁLYAUDVAR

NYUGATI PÁLYAUDVAR

TERÉZVÁROS

LIPÓTVÁROS

Néprajzi Múzeum

Országház

VÖRÖSMARTY UTCA

Terror Háza

KOSSUTH LAJOS TÉR

OKTOGON

ARANY JÁNOS UTCA

Operaház

OPERA

Szt. István Bazilika

BAJCSY ZSILINSZKY ÚT

Budavári palota

Széchenyi lánchíd

DEÁK FERENC TÉR

VÖRÖSMARTY TÉR

Nagy zsinagóga

BELVÁROS

Fővárosi Önkormányzat

ASTÓRIA

Tabáni plébániatemplom

FERENCIEK TERE

Belvárosi plébániatemplom

Ferences templom

Rác gyógyfürdő

Erzsébet híd

Petőfi Irodalmi Múzeum

Magyar Nemzeti Múzeum

KÁLVIN TÉR

Rudas gyógyfürdő

Citadella

Vásárcsarnok

Iparművészeti Múzeum

Szabadság híd

FERENCVÁROS

Gellért gyógyfürdő

Legend
- (i) Information
- ⊠ Post Office
- Ⓜ Metro Station
- Ⓗ HÉV Station
- 🚢 Boat Pier

0   1/4 mi
0   0.25 km

Bar Ladino **1**
Barokko Club & Lounge **2**
Buena Vista **3**
B7 **4**
Café Csiga **5**
Café Eklektika **6**
Capella **7**
Caledonian Scottish Pub **8**
Captain Cook **9**
Castro Bisztró **10**
Club Inside / Buddha Beach / Retro Beach **11**
Corvintető **12**
CoXx Men's Club **13**
Dürer kert **14**
Egri Borozó **15**
Ellátó **16**
Fat Mo's **17**
Fészek Club **18**
Gresham Bar **19**
Grinzingi **20**
Helvécia Söröző **21**
Incognito **22**
Instant **23**
Irish cat **24**
Jelen **25**
Katapult Café & Pub **26**
Kertem **27**
Kiadó Kocsma **28**
Kuplung **29**
L'enoteca **30**
Old Man's Music Pub **31**
Mumus **32**
Museum Cukrászda **33**
Negro **34**
Noiret **35**
Paris Texas **36**
Piaf **37**
Pótkulcs **38**
Sandokan Lisboa **39**
Sark **40**
Sirály **41**
Sixtus **42**
Szimplakert **43**
Szóda **44**
Tokaji Borozó **45**
Vittula **46**
Wichmann **47**

Islands Nightlife

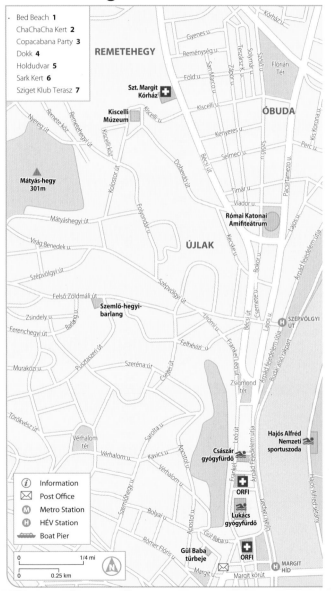

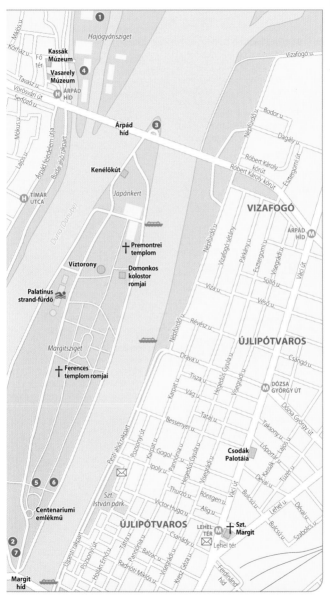

Hajógyárisziget

Kassák Múzeum

Vasarely Múzeum

ÁRPÁD HÍD

Árpád híd

Kenélőkút

Japánkert

Premontrei templom

Domonkos kolostor romjai

Víztorony

Palatinus strand-fürdő

Margitsziget

Ferences templom romjai

Centenáriumi emlékmű

Margit híd

VIZAFOGÓ

ÁRPÁD HÍD

ÚJLIPÓTVÁROS

DÓZSA GYÖRGY ÚT

Csodák Palotája

ÚJLIPÓTVÁROS

LEHEL TÉR

Szt. Margit

Lehel tér

Budapest Nightlife A to Z

Bars & Pubs

★★ Bambi Presszó BUDA
Named after a Socialist-period beverage, Bambi Presszó has original swinging Socialist sixties decor with red PVC and old guys playing dominos, plus a great terrace. Go early as it closes around 9pm. *Frankel Leó utca 2–4 (corner of Bem József utca).* ☎ *1/212-3171. Tram: 4/6 to Budai hídfő. Map p 111.*

★ Bar Ladino PEST Shabby cool bar-cum-eatery with funky brown wallpaper where old dudes playing cards in the afternoon give way to a thirty-something crowd. A good place to meet up before taking on the bars of Jewish District VII. *Dob utca 53.* ☎ *0630/874-3733. www. ladino.hu. Tram: 4/6 to Király utca. Map p 112.*

Barokko Club & Lounge PEST Three-level all-in-one cocktail lounge bar, club, and restaurant, plus a terrace onto the Pest party square of Liszt Ferenc tér. DJ parties downstairs. *Liszt Ferenc tér 5.* ☎ *1/322-0700. www.barokko.hu. Metro: M1 to Oktogon. Tram: 4/6 to Oktogon. Map p 112.*

★ Buena Vista PEST Trendy but classy with slick Nordic minimalist design, linseed oiled floors, mahogany tables, and a wide selection of drinks. Restaurant upstairs and great terrace right on fashionable Liszt Ferenc tér. *Liszt Ferenc tér 4–5.* ☎ *1/344-6303. Metro: M1 to Oktogon. Tram: 4/6 to Oktogon. Map p 112.*

★ Café Csiga PEST Cool Boho hangout with an intimate bar area at home on the corner of an atmospheric square. A good place to hang out at any time of day and food is also served. *Vásár utca 2.*

☎ *1/210-0885. Tram: 4/6 to Rákóczi tér. Map p 112.*

★★ Caledonian Scottish Pub PEST Draught Scottish bitter (or 'heavy' as it's known in Scotland), Belhaven Best flows freely in this cozy football-oriented gastropub that's noted for its all-day Scottish breakfast. It also has a Scottish gift shop should you get stuck watching the soccer and be needing a present to make amends. *Mozsár utca 9.* ☎ *1/311-7611. Metro: M1 to Oktogon. Tram: 4/6 to Oktogon. Map p 112.*

Captain Cook PEST While supposedly an English pub, in this respect it's far from authentic, being decked out in whatever memorabilia the owners could find. Nonetheless, this bar is hard to leave due to its intimate nooks and crannies, a cool terrace in summer, and terrific draught beer. *Bajcsy-Zsilinszky út 19/a.* ☎ *1/269-3136. Metro: M3 to Arany János utca. Map p 112.*

Castro Bisztró PEST The original Castro that lit up the trendy bar

Nordic minimalism at Buena Vista.

Fat Mo's speak-easy style.

strip of Ráday utca with its alternative vibe was a real favorite of mine, but the poster-laden new venue still comes up with the goods. The downside of its popularity is that the wonky wooden tables are often occupied. Decent Serbian food is on hand for sustenance. *Madách tér 3.* ☎ *1/215-0184. Metro: M1/M2/M3 to Deák tér. Map p 112.*

Déryné BUDA   This converted coffeehouse close to the Castle District, a favorite hangout of generally discerning and well-to-do thirty and ups, is a tasteful mix of trendy lounge room, cocktail and wine bar sections and also has a bistro, high end restaurant and breakfast joint all under one roof. *Krisztina tér 3.* ☎ *1/255-1407. Tram 18-56. Bus 105 to Krisztina tér. Map p 111.*

★★★ Ellátó PEST   Attracting a slightly older arty crowd, 'the bringer' delivers a lively and sometimes a tangibly flirty atmosphere. Stand around the bar and sip draught Staropramen, or decent wines by the glass, or retire to the seats in the backroom. Also features internationally influenced bar food. *Klauzál tér 2. No phone. Metro: M1 to Opera. Tram: 4/6 to Király utca. Map p 112.*

Fat Mo's PEST   A fun speak-easy style joint, it has a long bar and intimate dance floor. Fat Mo's is for those who want to avoid the big club experience but still want to get down and boogie. *Nyáry Pál utca 11.* ☎ *1/267-3199. Metro: M3 to Ferenciek tere or Kálvin tér. Map p 112.*

★★★ Gresham Bar PEST   Try the magical martinis in this pricey but classy cocktail bar, which adds grasshopper motives and an alabaster ceiling to Art Nouveau surroundings. *Four Seasons Gresham Palace Hotel, Roosevelt tér 5–6.* ☎ *1/268-5100. Metro: M1 to Vörösmarty tér. Tram: 2 to Roosevelt tér. Map p 112.*

Helvécia Söröző PEST   Atmospheric cellar pub but one that's clean, fun, and without the alcohol-inflicted grime so common in similar venues. Lots of 70s rock posters and music memorabilia, plus a pool table. *Eötvös utca 23/b.* ☎ *1/332-0207. Metro: M1 to Oktogon. Map p 112.*

★ Incognito PEST   Long-established favorite in über trendy Liszt Ferenc Square with more character than most. A fitting jazz soundtrack goes with the more discerning crowd but there's still a flirty edge. *Liszt Ferenc tér 3.* ☎ *1/342-1471. Metro: M1 to Oktogon. Tram: 4/6 to Oktogon. Map p 112.*

★★★ Instant PEST   This new kid on the alternative block is already drawing in hordes with its unique look and layout. Join the crowd in the covered courtyard or explore the nooks and crannies upstairs where you'll find several bars each with their own vibe. Look out for the dentist's chair. *Nagymező utca 38. Metro: M1 to Opera. Tram: 4/6 to Oktogon. Map p 112.*

Irish Cat PEST   A steamy weekend atmosphere warms up winter nights as dancing breaks out around

Old memorabilia adorns the walls at Lánchíd Söröző.

the bar fueled by an enthusiastic mixed age and nationality crowd. Guinness and food also served. *Múzeum körút 41.* ☎ *1/266-4085. Metro: M3 to Kálvin tér. Map p 112.*

★ **Jelen** PEST The 'Boys Don't Cry' poster by The Cure at the entrance of Jelen welcomes those looking to relive their student days. Serbian and Hungarian food is served. *Blaha Lujza tér 1–2 (corner of Márkus Emília utca and Stáhly utca).* ☎ *0626/344-3155. Metro: M2 to Blaha Lujza tér. Tram: 4/6. Map p 112.*

★ **Katapult Café & Pub** PEST Fun and colorful bar with DJ evenings, live music or just a Nirvana soundtrack. The terrace looks immediately out to the stunning Great Synagogue directly over the road. *Dohány utca 1.* ☎ *1/266-7226. Metro: M2 to Astoria. Map p 112.*

★★ **Kiadó Kocsma** PEST Cool hangout with an arty intellectual library booth-like setting downstairs and a bright street-level café upstairs. Decent pub grub, Magyar style. *Jókai tér 3.* ☎ *1/331-1955. Metro: M1 to Oktogon. Tram: 4/6 to Oktogon. Map p 112.*

★★ **Kuplung** PEST The 'Clutch' is a grungy underground Boho

hangout that was once a garage and still looks like one except for the very long bar, seats, and tables. Football tables and a ping-pong table are on hand for those up to the challenge. *Király utca 46.* ☎ *0630/986-8856. Metro: M1 to Opera. Map p 112.*

Lánchíd Söröző BUDA A great place for a beer after a hard day's Buda sightseeing. Simple and unpretentious, and decked out in old memorabilia, the welcome is a warm one. This was my favorite watering hole when I worked close by. *Fő utca 4.* ☎ *1/214-3144. Tram: 19 to to Clark Ádám tér. Bus: 86/105 to Clark Ádám tér. Map p 111.*

★ **Museum Cukrászda** PEST A busy cake and coffee shop by day, and by night a favorite of assorted revelers who come to sober up on solids—but often keep on drinking until the sun comes up. Cute terrace that's nice for seeing in the new day. *Múzeum körút 10.* ☎ *1/452-0888. Metro: M2 to Astoria.*

★★ **Negro** PEST Dark and sultry chichi lounge room/cocktail bar with a summer terrace leading onto the stunning basilica-dominated Szent István tér. The bar is actually located in the square's only ugly building, meaning you see the square at its best. *Szent István tér 11.* ☎ *1/302-0136. Metro: M1 to Bajcsy-Zsilinszky út. Map p 112.*

Noiret PEST   Pool and darts cellar with a party vibe and a jukebox pumping out greatest hits soundtracks. It also has a single snooker table and a separate non-smoking pool area. *Dessewffy utca 8–10 (corner of Hajos utca).* ☎ *1/331-6103. Metro: M3 to Arany János utca. Map p 112.*

Old Man's Music Pub PEST Good late on for a last drink and a free dance to old classics, or for local rock gigs. The mature female clientele make this music pub just as much the 'Old Girl's' as the 'Old Man's'. *Akácfa utca 13.* ☎ *1/322-7645. Metro: M2 to Blaha Lujza tér. Tram: 4/6. Map p 112.*

★★ **Oscar Café** BUDA   A city slickers-oriented Buda bar that's known for top cocktails, good wine, and draught beer, which pardons the now-dated Hollywood theme that, fortunately, is hidden with the dim lighting. *Ostrom utca 14.* ☎ *1/212-8017. Metro: M2 to Moszkva tér. Tram: 4/6. Map p 111.*

★ **Paris Texas** PEST   An old favorite on the trendy Ráday utca party strip, whose venues often lack substance over style. Here, however, the pictures on the wall of

friendly faces are welcoming as you settle down for a drink in this real pub atmosphere. The seats outside are pleasant too. *Ráday utca 22.* ☎ *1/218-0570. Metro: M3 to Kálvin tér. Tram: 47/49. Map p 112.*

★ **Paulaner Brauhaus** BUDA   A huge German gastro beer hall with beer brewed on site, and the fact it's in a shopping mall hardly detracts from the experience. Wheat beer is búzasör in Hungarian, but the staff will understand German 'weißbier'. *Top floor of MOM Park, Alkotás utca 53.* ☎ *1/224-2020. Tram: 61 to Csörsz utca. Map p 111.*

★ **Pótkulcs** PEST   Set behind a nondescript gate, the 'Spare Key' is easy to miss but difficult to leave. Tavern-like on one side by the bar, Pótkulcs becomes a grungy cellar on the other. Popular with the student and young alternative crowd, it also serves plenty of veggie pub grub. *Csengery utca 65/B.* ☎ *1/269-1050. Metro: M3 to Nyugati pu. Tram: 4/6 to Nyugati pu. Map p 112.*

★★ **Sandokan Lisboa** PEST The colorfully tiled interior and decaying townhouses on this pedestrian street, onto which the action spills in summer, conjure up the city of Lisbon. There may be no Portuguese beer but the thirst-quenching draught Spanish San Miguel is close enough. *Hajós utca 23 (corner*

Museum Cukrászda.

of Ó utca). ☎ 1/302-7002. Metro: M1 to Opera. Map p 112.

★★★ **Sark** PEST I've dropped into the cool 'Corner Bar' many times to meet up with friends before embarking on a tour of District VII nightspots only to spend the whole evening there. Chat up upstairs, chill out in the gallery or groove to music down in the basement. Usually attracts an alternative/student crowd. *Klauzál tér 14. ☎ 1/328-0753. Tram: 4/6 to Király utca. Map p 112.*

★ **Sirály** PEST A twisty staircase connects this three-level arty venue that's everything from a buzzing bar-cum-coffee house, to a concert and theater venue, internet hotspot, exhibition space, and occasional cinema. *Király utca 50. ☎ 0620/957-2291. Tram: 4/6 to Király utca. Map p 112.*

★★ **Sixtus** PEST Tiny bar with a big personality, it's a longtime home to boho expats and likeminded arty Hungarians. Slightly cliquey at first sight, but everyone's your friend when the drinks start to flow. *Nagy Diófa utca 26–28. ☎ 1/413-6722. Metro: M2 to Blaha Lujza tér. Tram: 4/6 to Wesselényi utca. Map p 112.*

★★★ **Szimplakert** PEST The great survivor of temporary nightspots that sprung up in derelict

Admire the Manga wallpaper at Szóda.

buildings has made this, its second location, its permanent home. Shabby cool and expanding, with free WiFi it seems to be many people's unofficial office. *Kazinczy utca 14. No phone. Metro: M2 to Blaha Lujza Astoria. Bus: 7 to Uránia. Map p 112.*

★★ **Szóda** PEST The alternative ambience here is provided by a backdrop of Japanese Manga comic strip wallpaper, retro red plastic seats, and soda siphons, attracting a young arty crowd. There's a fun dance floor downstairs in fall and winter. *Wesselényi utca 18. ☎ 0670/389-6463. Tram: 4/6 to Wesselényi utca. Metro: M2 to Astoria. Map p 112.*

★★ **Vittula** PEST Grungy hip cellar bar frequented by a friendly and up-for-it mixed nationality clientele. The alternative rock soundtrack is supplemented by occasional DJs. Ask at the bar about Vittula's art gallery. *Kertész utca 4. No phone. Metro: M2 to Blaha Lujza tér. Map p 112.*

★ **Wichmann** PEST Classic smoky drinking den in a lovely old house that, along with the long wooden tables and bar, give it an old-world tavern feel. Cheap wine, beer, and spirits are consumed by the eclectic crowd with remarkable speed. *Kazinczy utca 55. ☎ 1/322-6174. Tram: 4 or 6 to Király utca. Map p 112.*

Wine Bars

★★ **Andante** BUDA Serious wine bar in an elegant riverside building next to the Chain Bridge offering an extensive selection of Hungarian wines with cold dishes to match. Founders include winemaker Zsolt Tiffán and the pop star Ákos. *Bem rakpart 2. ☎ 1/457-0807. Closed Sun & Mon. Metro: M2 to Batthány tér. Map p 111.*

Egri Borozó PEST Unpretentious wine cellar with Flintstone furniture selling barrels of cheap and cheerful vino in green ceramic jugs and mugs. Not sure if it's the quantity or quality that gives the next-day headache—but that's a small price to pay. *Bajcsy-Zsilinszky út 72.* ☎ *1/302-1724. Metro: M3 to Nyugati pu. or Arany János utca. Tram: 4/6 to Nyugati pu. Map p 112.*

Grinzingi PEST Rough-and-ready wine bar with a great atmosphere where five different types of wine from the Mátra region flow in a scary quantity. The chairs are chunky and fixed to the floor so nobody falls off. *Veres Pálné utca 10.* ☎ *1/317-4624. Metro: M3 to Ferenciek tere. Map p 112.*

★★ L'enoteca PEST Cute Italianate wine bar with a wide selection of quality Hungarian and Italian wines available by the glass and bottle, plus cheese, hams, and salumis. Great views to Buda from the street terrace. *Belgrád rakpart 13.* ☎ *1/486-1665. Tram: 2 to Március 15. tér. Map p 112.*

Mátravidéki Borozó BUDA Hardened local drinkers occupy the front bar area downing the cheap but quaffable wine from the Mátra. The lady of the house keeps the place in tip-top condition and the cool rustic back room is very pleasant. *Corvin tér 1.* ☎ *1/214-4020. Metro: M2 to Batthyány tér. Map p 111.*

★ Tokaji Borozó PEST Descend the steps into this crypt-like setting

Find an extensive selection of Hungarian wines at Andante.

that swallows up people from all walks of life heading home from work. You certainly won't find the finest examples of the sumptuously sweet Tokaji Aszú here (see p 150) but you will find a great wine cellar atmosphere and some hearty bites. *Falk Miksa utca 32.* ☎ *1/269-3143. Tram: 2/4/6 to Jászai Mari tér. Map p 112.*

Summer Bars/Venues
★★★ Bed Beach HAJÓ-GYÁRISZIGET Whiter than white décor, the ideal backdrop for hot hedonistic nights to hardcore dance music on Budapest's glitzy nightlife island. The place to be seen but not for a quiet drink. *Hajógyárisziget.* ☎ *0630/436-4400. Suburban train: HÉV to Filatorigát. Map p 114.*

Garden Party

The hot summer bars and venues are usually open May to September but sometimes open later due to bad weather. Many come and go but the once listed are expected to be open in 2009 and beyond.

★★ **Cafe del Rio** BUDA   Dress in your summer coolest and sip expensive cocktails at this fancy outdoor venue that pumps out dance music to a backdrop of palm trees and undeniably beautiful girls. *Goldmann György tér 1.* ☎ *0630/297-2158. www.rio.hu. No cover Mon–Thur. Ft 1,000 cover Fri–Sat after 11pm. Tram: 4/6 to Petőfi híd budai hídfő. Map p 111.*

ChaChaCha Kert MARGARET ISLAND   Sandwiched between tennis courts and a sports stadium, this outdoor venue goes from a relaxed place to take an early evening drink to groove central as everyone takes to the al fresco dance floor (on hot summer nights from Wednesday to Saturday). After summer the action moves indoors and underground to a cool cellar labyrinth at Bajcsy Zsilinszky út 63, close to Nuygati Station. *Tram: 4/ 6 to Margitsziget. Bus: 26 to Szigeti bejáró. Map p 114.*

Copacabana Party MARGARET ISLAND   Copacabana hosts regular gigs at its pleasant riverside spot. Take your drinks to the northern tip of the island and hang off like Di Caprio and Winslet in the movie *Titanic. Margitsziget (entrance*

from island under Árpád bridge). ☎ *1/239-1509. Bus: 26 to Zenélőkút. Map p 114.*

★★★ **Corvintető** PEST   Set atop a Socialist-era shopping complex, Corvin is a cool spot on steamy summer nights. The rooftop is open summers only but the Bohemian warehouse-type hangout is worth checking out any time of the year. (You'll need to climb several flights of stairs.) *Corvin Áruház; Blaha Lujza tér 1–2 (entrance from Somogyi Béla utca).* ☎ *0620/772-2984. Metro: M2 to Blaha Lujza tér. Tram: 4/6 to Blaha Lujza tér.*

★★ **Dürer kert** PEST   Drink and think in this cool, less-frequented courtyard of the Arts University. Tree stumps, colorful lights plus DJs and gigs at weekends with a fun interior maze of extreme retro rooms that are also open winters. *Ajtósi Dürer sor 19–21.* ☎ *1/789-4444. Trolley bus: 74 to Ajtósi Dürer sor. Map p 112.*

★★ **Fecske** BUDA   Relaxing and airy rooftop location with cushioned sofas overlooking the Komjádi swimming pool. The aquatic theme continues with views down the Danube and sun beds. Food served.

Trendy nightspot Holdudvar.

Árpád fejedelem útja 8. ☎ *1/326-0714. Bus: 6/60/86 to Császár-Komjádi Uszoda. Map p 111.*

★★★ **Holdudvar** MARGARET ISLAND   Converted from a famous casino, this trendy nightspot successfully marries old-world charm with modern touches. The garden bars are surrounded by trees, plus there's a gallery, dance floor, and a restaurant. ☎ *1/236-0155. Tram: 4/6 to Margitsziget. Bus: 26 to Hajós Alfréd Uszoda. Map p 114.*

★★ **Kertem** PEST   The extremely laid back 'My Garden' feels like everyone's garden. Old vinyl discs decorate the bar, while the sleeves of incredibly schmaltzy looking singers line the route to the toilets. Christmas lights add funky color after dark. *Olof Palme sétány 3. Metro: M1 to Hősök tere. Map p 112.*

★★★ **Mumus** PEST   After a four-year absence, Mumus returned in 2008 with its unique brand of alternative art and decor that has been applied to this once derelict Jewish District townhouse. Colorful entrance, installations, and a gallery next to the toilet. *Dob utca 18. No phone. Metro: M2 to Astoria. Map p 112.*

★★ **Romkert** BUDA   Dramatically situated between the river and the foot of Gellért Hill, in the garden under the beautiful Turkish dome of the Rudás baths. There's always a steady flow of cocktails and the music scene is set for a serious al fresco party. *Döbrentei tér 9 (Garden of the Rudas Baths). Tram: 18/19 to Döbrentei tér. Map p 111.*

★ **kids Sark Kert** MARGARET ISLAND   Next to the Danube bank on Margaret Island, this laidback, slightly grungy and bamboo-laden setting is ideal for a quiet drink and a chat under the sun or stars. The light shines enticingly off the

Mumus.

Danube at night, but the toilets aren't that idyllic. Kids' play area. *Tram: 4/6 to Margitsziget. Map p 114.*

Sziget Klub Terasz MARGARET ISLAND   Overlooking my favorite tennis courts (p 89) and perched above the Danube this is an enjoyable place for a quiet drink without grunge or glamour. *Margitsziget (approx. 100m on left entering island from Margaret Bridge).* ☎ *0670/531-2955. Tram: 4/6 to Margitsziget. Map p 114.*

Zöld Pardon BUDA   Festival-like atmosphere attracting an up-for-it student crowd. Varied attractions include a lake bar you paddle up to, a pálinka (fruit brandy) house, a games and dance area plus loads of live music. *Southern side of Goldmann György tér. Tram: 4/6 to Petőfi hid, Budai hidfő. Map p 111.*

Clubs

★★ **B7** PEST   Big booming 'rhythm and bling' dance club in the heart of central Pest providing glitzy nightlife action without having to trek out to the big clubs of Hajogyári Sziget. *Nagymező utca 48–48.* ☎ *1/269-0573. www.b7.hu.*

Admission varies. Open Wed–Sat. Metro: M1 to Oktogon or Opera. Map p 112.

★★ Club Inside/Buddha Beach/Retro Beach PEST
Pest waterfront and riverside warehouses converted and devoted to good times. House, techno, and disco, plus old classics are churned out. In summer, the party moves to retro-style Buddha Beach and Retro Beach. *Közraktár utca 9–11.* ☎ *1/210-4872. www.clubinside.hu. Entry to Club Inside Ft 1,500 for men, women free. Open Fri, Sat. Free entry to Buddha Beach/Retro Beach, open every day May–Sep. Tram: 2 to Közraktár utca. Map p 112.*

★★★ Dokk HAJÓGYÁRISZIGET
Über trendy club with top dance DJs in a spacious converted warehouse on Hajogyári Sziget (Boatyard Island). The sight of so many beautiful girls under one roof gets the men's pulses racing. The action moves outdoors to Dock Beach in summer. *Hajógyárisziget 122.* ☎ *0630/535-2747. Entry varies. Dokk Beach free entry. Suburban train: HÉV to Filatorigát. Map p 114.*

★★★ Fészek Club PEST
Amazing bijou artists' cellar club with a risqué atmosphere and borderline bordello decoration. However, you never know what you're going to get here—it ranges from seriously arty one night to gangster bling the next. *Kertész utca 36.* ☎ *1/342-6549. Free–Ft 300 cover. Tram: 4/6 to Kiraly utca. Map p 112.*

★★★ Piaf PEST
This Budapest classic rocks through till dawn with Parisian-style sleaze upstairs and a greatest hits soundtrack downstairs. The slightly mature crowd should know better but can't resist coming back. Ring the bell to get in. *Nagymező utca 25.* ☎ *1/312-3823. www.piafklub.hu. Ft 800 cover, including one drink. Metro: M1 to Oktogon or Opera. Tram: 4/6 to Oktogon. Map p 112.*

Gay & Lesbian

★★ Café Eklektika PEST
The same old lovely lesbian hospitality as its like-named predecessor now comes in a more mature location and under a stucco ceiling. A great hangout any time of day. *Nagymező utca 30.* ☎ *1/266-1266. www. eklektika.hu. Metro: M1 to Oktogon or Opera. Map p 112.*

★★ Capella PEST
This Pest three-level waterfront hotspot is a bit too mixed for some as many straights pile in for the midnight drag show. Nevertheless, a lively crowd twists the night away to dance and disco in camped-up surroundings. *Belgrád rakpart 23.* ☎ *1/318-6231. wwww.capella.hu. Admission varies. Wed–Sat. Tram: 2 to Március 15 tér. Map p 112.*

★★★ CoXx Men's Club PEST
Hidden gents' club with themed nights including macho, military cruising, and a 'bear club'. Tastefully done but quite hardcore. *Dohány utca 38.* ☎ *1/344-4884. www.coxx.hu. Ft 1,000 admission. Metro: M2 to Blaha Lujza tér. Map p 112.* ●

Arts & Entertainment Best Bets

Best **Art Nouveau Auditorium**
★★★ Ferenc Liszt Music Academy (Liszt Ferenc Zeneakadémia), *Liszt Ferenc tér 8 (p 132)*

Best **Collection of European Masters**
★★★ Fine Arts Museum, *Dózsa György út 41. Overlooking Heroes Square (p 130)*

Best **Contemporary Performance Art**
★★★ Trafó House of Contemporary Arts, *Liliom utca 41 (p 134)*

Best **Floating Rock Concerts**
★★★ A38 Ship, *Moored on the River Danube next to Petőfi híd (p 133)*

Best **Folk Concerts**
★★★ Fonó Budai Zeneház, *Sztregova utca 3 (p 134)*

Best **Free Underground Concerts**
★★★ Gödör, *Erzsébet tér. (p 14)*

Best **Heavenly Acoustics**
★★★ Matthias Church (Mátyás Templom), *Szentháromság tér 2 (p 132)*

Best **Independent and Gay Movies**
Cirko-geyzir, *Balassi Bálint utca 15–17 (p 133)*

Best **Magyar Masters**
★★★ National Gallery, *Buda Palace, Buildings A, B, C, D. Szent György tér 2 (p 131)*

Best **Night at the Opera**
★★★ Opera House, *Andrássy út 22 (p 133)*

Best **Pop Art**
★ Ludwig Museum, *Palace of Arts, Komor Marcell utca (p 130)*

Best **State-of-the-Art Classic Music Venue**
★★ Béla Bartók National Concert Hall, *Palace of Arts. Komor Marcell utca (p 132)*

Best Place to **Tap into the Local Jazz Scene**
★ Columbus Jazz Club, *Permanently moored on the River Danube at Vigadó tér (p 134)*

Matthias Church for heavenly acoustics.

Buda Arts & Entertainment

A38 Ship **1**
Fonó Budai Zeneház **2**
Matthias Church **3**
Millenáris **4**
National Dance Theatre **5**
National Gallery **6**
Óbudai Társakör **7**

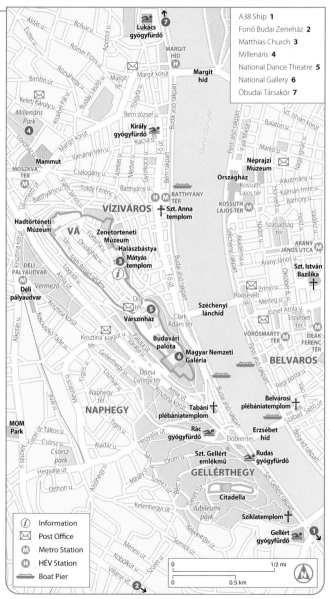

Information
Post Office
Metro Station
HÉV Station
Boat Pier

Pest Arts & Entertainment

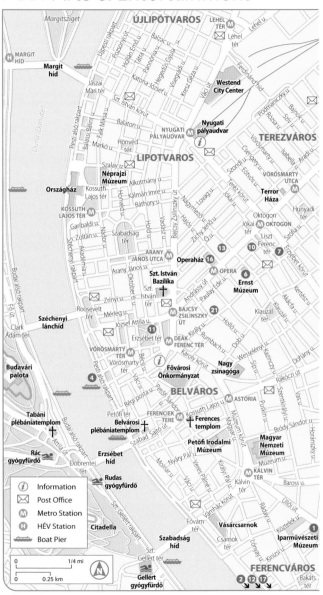

Margitsziget

ÚJLIPÓTVÁROS

LEHEL TÉR

Lehel u.

Lehel tér

MARGIT HÍD

Margit híd

Jászai Mari tér

Westend City Center

Váci út

TERÉZVÁROS

Duna (Danube)

NYUGATI PÁLYAUDVAR

Nyugati pályaudvar

LIPÓTVÁROS

Néprajzi Múzeum

Országház

KOSSUTH LAJOS TÉR

VÖRÖSMARTY UTCA

Terror Háza

OKTOGON

Liszt Ferenc tér

ARANY JÁNOS UTCA

Operaház 16

OPERA

Szt. István Bazilika

Ernst Múzeum 6

Széchenyi lánchíd

BAJCSY ZSILINSZKY ÚT 21

Budavári palota

DEÁK FERENC TÉR

VÖRÖSMARTY TÉR

Fővárosi Önkormányzat

Nagy zsinagóga

Tabáni plébániatemplom

BELVÁROS

ASTORIA

FERENCIEK TERE

Ferences templom

Belvárosi plébániatemplom

Rác gyógyfürdő

Erzsébet híd

Petőfi Irodalmi Múzeum

Magyar Nemzeti Múzeum

KÁLVIN TÉR

Rudas gyógyfürdő

(i)	Information
✉	Post Office
Ⓜ	Metro Station
Ⓗ	HÉV Station
⛴	Boat Pier

Citadella

Vásárcsarnok

Iparművészeti Múzeum 1

Szabadság híd

0 ——— 1/4 mi
0 ——— 0.25 km

Gellért gyógyfürdő

FERENCVÁROS

2 12 17

Applied Arts Museum **1**
Béla Bartók National Concert Hall **2**
Budapest Arena **3**
Columbus Jazz Club **4**
Erkel Színház **5**
Ernst Museum **6**
Ferenc Liszt Music Academy **7**
Filter Klub **8**
Fine Arts Museum **9**
Giero **10**
Gödör **11**
Ludwig Museum **12**
Mai Manó Gallery **13**
Műcsarnok **14**
Nádor Terem **15**
Opera House **16**
Palace of Arts **17**
PECSA **18**
Trafó Bár Tangó **19**
Trafó House of Contemporary Arts **20**
VAM Design Center **21**

Arts & Entertainment **A to Z**

Art Galleries & Museums

★★★ Applied Arts Museum

PEST   Porcelain once owned by the Tsars, Habsburgs, and a bizarre singing saint from Madrid star among Art Nouveau objets indus-triels. The museum also features many temporary exhibitions and is a good place to take kids who can join interactive educational searches (see p 115, bullet ⑧). *Üllői út 33–37. Metro: M3 to Ferenc körút. Map p 128.*

Ernst Museum

PEST   Temporary exhibition space that's run by the Műcsarnok, which focuses on 'the-matic solo and group exhibitions that reflect on the social and urban environment'. Anything from local to Mexican artists can be exhibited. *Nagymező utca 8. ☎ 1/460-7000. www.mucsarnok.hu. Tickets Ft 1,200. Metro: M1 to Opera. Map p 128.*

★★★ Fine Arts Museum

PEST   An outstanding collection of Span-ish masters (see p 14, bullet ❸) plus other greats including Raphael, Titian, Tiepolo, Brueghel the Elder, Van Dyck, Jordaens, Rembrandt, Reynolds, Constable, and the part-Hungarian Dürer whose father hailed from Hungary. 🕐 *1½–2 hr. Come early when major temporary exhibitions are running. Dózsa György út 41. Overlooking Heroes Square. ☎ 1/469 7100. www.szepmuveszeti.hu. Ft 1,200. Tues–Sun 10am–5:30pm. Metro: M1 to Hősök tere.*

★ Ludwig Museum

PEST   Lichtenstein, Warhol, and a Picasso matador carousing with a naked woman feature among contempo-rary Magyar artists and their works. *Palace of Arts, Komor Marcell utca 1. ☎ 1/555-3444. www.ludwigmuseum.hu. Free for permanent collection. Tram: 2 to Millenniumi Kulturális Központ. Map p 128.*

Mai Manó Gallery

PEST   Photographer Manó Mai is the man behind this suitably arty 1894 build-ing. Home to the Hungarian Founda-tion of Photography, it hosts varied local and international photo exhibi-tions. Chic adjoining bar. *Nagymező utca 20. ☎ 1/473-2666. www.maimano.hu. Tickets Ft 700. Metro: M1 to Opera. Map p 128.*

Mai Manó Gallery, home to the Hungarian Foundation of Photography.

From Station to Station

An argument has ensued over the gleaming frescoes that adorn the main waiting room at Keleti, Budapest's neo-Baroque Eastern train station. Dating back to 1884, but immaculately restored in 2008, much of the rest of the station, which is palatial in design and dramatic in dimension, is pretty run down. Step into the international ticket office to see the contrast or check the outside of the building. The centerpiece features mythological figures sitting on a rail car and pulled by angels down the tracks. It is flanked by further elaborate paintings depicting the pillars of economy. Eiffel's Nyugati Station is an epic glass and iron structure that commuters barely notice as they pile into Pest on their way to work. One of the side buildings is home to a remarkably grand McDonalds. Otherwise, nightclubs take up this prime space. For an excellent view from up above, climb the stairs of the Skala shopping center opposite. In 2008 a roof-top bar was operating.

★★ **Műcsarnok** PEST   Behind the striking exterior of this neo-Renaissance building lies a top exhibition space, which holds up to six major local and international contemporary visual art exhibitions annually. *Hősök tere.* ☎ *1/460-7014. www.mucsarnok.hu. Tickets Ft 1,200. Metro: M1 to Hősök tere. Map p 128.*

★★★ **National Gallery** BUDA Look out for works by the darkly talented Mihály Munkácsy, the completely unique Tivadar Csontváry, who Picasso once referred to as the other great artist of the 20th century, and Hungary's very own Impressionist Rippl-Rónai. *Buda Palace, Buildings A, B, C, D. Szent György tér 2. www.mng.hu.* ☎ *0620/439-7420. Tickets Ft 800. Bus: 16/16A/116 to Dísz tér. Map p 127.*

Arts Centers
★★★ kids **Millenáris** BUDA Über cool converted industrial complex packed with urban art, installations, and holds film festivals, concerts and DJ nights.

It's so diverse that nothing would surprise me. Nice outdoor area for kids. *Kis Rókus utca 16–20.* ☎ *1/336-4000. www.millenaris.hu. Tickets vary. Metro: M2 to Moszkva tér. Tram: 4/6 to Széna tér. Map p 127.*

Palace of Arts (Művészetek Palotája) PEST   This high-tech and chic art house is the centerpiece of the new 'Millennium City Center' with the Ludwig Gallery, Béla Bartók National Concert Hall, and Festival Theater among its attractions. *Komor Marcell utca 1.* ☎ *1/555-3001. Tram: 2 to Millenniumi Kulturális Központ. Map p 128.*

★★★ **Trafó House of Contemporary Arts** PEST   This hotbed of cutting-edge expression plays host to a variety of local and international performance arts, many of which are accessible for non-Hungarian speakers. *Liliom utca 41.* ☎ *1/215-1600. www.trafo.hu. Tickets vary. Metro: M2 to Ferenc Körút. Map p 128.*

★★ VAM Design Center PEST Impressive new arts center that hosted the internationally renowned Bodies exhibition in 2008. Its revolving exhibitions by local artists are dramatically displayed around the covered courtyard of this former townhouse as well as in the side rooms that were once apartments. The pictures can be bought. *Király utca 26.* ☎ *1/666-3141. www.vam design.hu. Tickets vary, courtyard exhibitions free. Tram: 4/6 to Király utca. Map p 128.*

Classical Music Venues
★★ Béla Bartók National Concert Hall PEST Home to the Hungarian Philharmonic Orchestra led by the world-famous pianist Zoltán Kocsis, this state-of-the-art venue has the same dimensions as a Gothic cathedral and the acoustics to match. *Palace of Arts, Komor Marcell utca 1.* ☎ *1/555-3300. Tickets vary. Tram: 2 to Millenniumi Kulturális Központ. Map p 128.*

Erkel Színház PEST Socialist-realist from the outside, but pleasing acoustics from the inside. Although I once saw Nick Cave and the Bad Seeds here, it's used mainly to share Budapest's opera and ballet burden with the Opera House and Thalia Theater. *Köztársaság tér 30.* ☎ *1/333-0540. www.opera.hu. Tickets vary. Metro: M2 to Blaha Luiza tér. Map p 128.*

★★★ Ferenc Liszt Music Academy (Liszt Ferenc Zeneakadémia) PEST Facing funding cuts, this 130-year-old education institution is paying for itself by putting on more of its own concerts, featuring the cream of Hungarian talent. Regular performances are held in the awesome Art Nouveau auditorium. An experience not to be missed. See p 24, bullet **7**. *Liszt Ferenc tér 8.* ☎ *1/342-0179. Tickets vary. Metro: M1 to Oktogon. Tram: 4/6 Oktogon. Map p 128.*

★★★ Matthias Church (Mátyás Templom) BUDA Heavenly surroundings and acoustics make for an outstanding classical music experience. The kind of place that is built to handle all that Handel's *Messiah* can throw at it. *Szentháromság tér 2.* ☎ *1/355-5657. www.matyastemplom.hu. Tickets vary. Bus: 16/16A/116 to Szentháromság tér. Map p 127.*

★★ Nádor Terem PEST The intimate bijou Art Nouveau Nádor Hall, hidden away in the Institute of the Blind, is a prime venue for strings, chamber music, and virtuoso performances. *Ajtósi Dürer sor 39.* ☎ *1/ 344-7072. Closed Jul & Aug.*

VAM Design Center.

Tickets on sale before performance, price varies. Metro: M1 to Mexikói út. Map p 128.

★★ **Óbudai Társakör** ÓBUDA The Franz Liszt Chamber Orchestra, Budapest Strings, and Auer String Quartet are regulars at this wonderfully restored enclave of 'Old Buda', sadly a gatecrasher these days in the realm of high rises. 'Music in the Garden' in summer. *Kiskorona utca 7.* ☎ *1/250-0288. www.obudai tarsaskor.hu. Tickets vary. Suburban train: HÉV to Árpád híd. Map p 127.*

★★★ **Opera House** PEST At the cutting edge when it was opened by Franz Joseph I in 1884, both in terms of design and functionality, the Opera House is desperate to replace the creaking East German stage and concrete pit to restore the once-outstanding acoustics. She still looks beautiful though, and the great-value opera and ballet is a must. (See p 8, bullet ❸.) *Andrássy út 22.* ☎ *153-0170 for tickets. www.opera.hu. Metro: M1 to Opera.*

Dance

★★ **National Dance Theatre** BUDA Ballet, folk, modern, and contemporary dance on tap in this handsome theater, itself very much part of the beauty of the Castle District. *Színház utca 1–3.* ☎ *1/201-4407. www.dancetheatre.hu. Tickets vary. Bus: 16/16A/116 to Dísz tér. Map p 127.*

Live Music

★★★ **A38 Ship** RIVER DANUBE Local and international acts, including names as big as John Cale on this very hip Ukrainian ship. Industrial cool bar in the engine room and swanky restaurant top deck. *Moored next to Petőfi híd (Petőfi Bridge).* ☎ *1/464-3940. www. a38.hu. Tickets vary. Closed Sun. Tram: 4/6 to Petőfi híd, budai hídfő. Map p 127.*

Budapest Arena PEST The multipurpose Papp László Budapest Sport Arena, to give this huge spaceship-like building its full name, replaced an older venue that burnt down, and sadly wasn't in place to

Movie Marvels

While the shopping mall cinemas are comfy and kitted out with state-of-the-art movie technology—Arena Plaza (see p 78) even has a VIP area—Budapest is also home to some cool art-house cinemas and handsome old relics from the golden age of cinema. Művész (Teréz körút 30. ☎ 1/332-6726) screens a wide range of mainly less-commercial films, new and not so new. Örökmozgó (Erzsébet körút 39. ☎ 1/342-2167) and Cirko-geyzir (Balassi Bálint utca 15–17. ☎ 1/269-1915) are seriously offbeat while the Moorish-influenced Uránia (Rákóczi út 21. ☎ 1/486-3413) has been restored to its fin-de-siècle splendor and has viewing boxes that make for a special experience. Both the mall and arthouse types of *mozi* (cinema) show plenty of films in English. The weekly *Budapest Sun* has cinema listings and English language portal Xpatloop.com has a search function.

host the likes of Guns 'n' Roses in their heyday. However, there are plenty of their present-day comtemporaries: fellow stadium rockers Coldplay made it here in fall 2008. ☎ *1/422-2600. www.budapest arena.hu. Tickets vary. Metro: M2 to Stadionok. Map p 128.*

★ **Columbus Jazz Club** DANUBE This is the place to tap into the local jazz scene. Prices for drinks, however, are high on this slightly cheaplooking floating jazz venue, but the music makes up for it. *Permanently moored close to Vigadó tér.* ☎ *1/266-9013. Tickets vary. Tram: 2 to Vigadó tér. Map p 128.*

Filter Klub PEST Absolutely no filtering of the end product goes on in this raw hard rock hangout. Plenty of young punk bands strut their stuff for free, especially on school nights. *Almássy utca 1.* ☎ *0630/921-4212. Free entry. Metro: M2 to Blaha Lujza tér. Tram: 4/6 to Wesselényii utca or Blaha Lujza tér. Map p 128.*

★★★ **Fonó Budai Zeneház** BUDA Top Hungarian and Transylvanian folk acts on Wednesdays, with powerful and unrestrained Csángó, a folk style from a Hungarian minority hailing from deepest Romania and Moldavia. Gypsy dance classes, too. *Sztregova utca 3.* ☎ *1/206-5300. www.fono.hu.*

Tickets vary. Tram: 47 to Kalotaszeg utca. Map p 127.

★★ **Giero** PEST Tiny cellar place where Gypsy Jazz musicians meet up to jam and hang out. Electric atmosphere and decent rustic cooking. Free, but a few tips get them to really go for it. *Paulay Ede utca 56. Free entry. Metro: M1 to Oktogon. Map p 128.*

★★★ **Gödör** PEST Weird, wonderful, and varied program of concerts sees all the beats from across the globe sounding in this stylish subterranean setting under Erszebet tér. Local gypsy greats Romano Drom are a feature. Nice outdoor bit. *Erzsébet tér.* ☎ *0620/201-3868. www.godorklub.hu. Tickets vary, often no cover charge. Metro: M1/M2/M3 to Deák tér. Map p 128.*

PECSA PEST This retro kitsch venue attracts the likes of big lesscommercial stars like Morrissey and Nick Cave. (See p 48, bullet ⑧.)

★★★ **Trafó Bár Tangó** PEST The cellar club of the truly progressive Trafó unsurprisingly pulls in many budding alternative bands, plus the likes of legendary Creation Records founder Alan McGee who has a residency here with his Death Disco. *Liliom utca 41.* ☎ *1/456-2053. www.trafo.hu. Tickets vary. Metro: M3 to Ferenc körút. Tram: 4/6 to Ferenc körút. Map p 128.* ●

The multi-purpose Budapest Arena.

Lodging Best Bets

Best **Art Deco Hotel**
★★ Andrássy Hotel MaMaison
$$–$$$$ *Andrassy út 111 (p 140)*

Best **Art Nouveau Hotel**
★★★ Four Seasons Hotel
Gresham Palace Budapest
$$$$–$$$$$ *Roosevelt tér 5–6*
(p 142)

Best **Bargain View**
Citadella Hotel $ *Citadella sétány*
(p 141)

Best **Boutique Hotel**
★★ Zara Boutique Hotel $$–$$$
Só utca 6 (p 144)

Best **Cheap 'n' Cheerful
Socialist-era Lodgings**
Medosz $ *Jókai tér 9 (p 144)*

Best **Designer Hotel**
★★★ Lánchíd 19 $$–$$$ *Lánchíd*
utca 19–21 (p 143)

Best **Old World Ambience**
★★ Danubius Hotel Astoria $$
Kossuth Lajos utca 19–21 (p 142);
★★ Danubius Hotel Gellért $–$$$
Szent Gellért tér 1 (p 142)

Best **Restored Old Favorites**
★★★ Boscolo New York Palace
$$–$$$$$ *Erzsébet 9–11 (p 140)*;
★★★ Corinthia Grand Royal Hotel
$$–$$$$ *Erzsébet körút 43–49*
(p 141)

Best **Spa Hotels**
★★ Danubius Health Spa Resort
Margitsziget $$ *Margitsziget*
(Margaret Island) (p 141); ★ Danubius
Health Spa Resort Helia $$ *Kárpát*
utca 62–64 (p 141); ★ Ramada Plaza
$$–$$$$$ *Árpád fejedelem útja 94*
(p 144)

The Boscolo New York Palace.

Best **Views**
★★ Marriott $$–$$$ *Apáczai*
Csere János utca 4 (Map p 144);
★★★ Four Seasons Hotel
Gresham Palace Budapest
$$$$–$$$$$ *Roosevelt tér 5–6*
(p 142); ★★ Sofitel Budapest
Maria Dorottya $$–$$$$$
Roosevelt tér 2–9 (p 144)

Best **Villa**
★ Uhu Villa, *Kesely utca 1 (p 144)*

Best **When Money is No
Object**
★★★ Four Seasons Hotel Gresham
Palace Budapest $$$$–$$$$$
Roosevelt tér 5–6 (p 142)

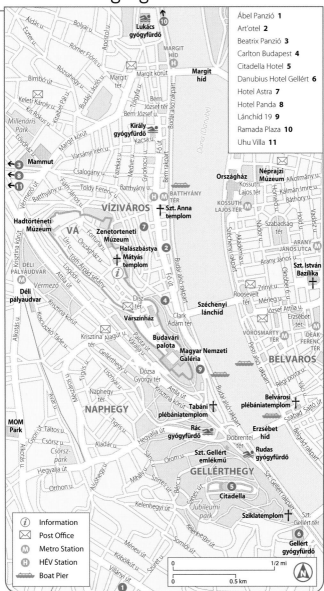

Buda Lodging

Ábel Panzió **1**
Art'otel **2**
Beatrix Panzió **3**
Carlton Budapest **4**
Citadella Hotel **5**
Danubius Hotel Gellért **6**
Hotel Astra **7**
Hotel Panda **8**
Lánchíd 19 **9**
Ramada Plaza **10**
Uhu Villa **11**

Pest Lodging

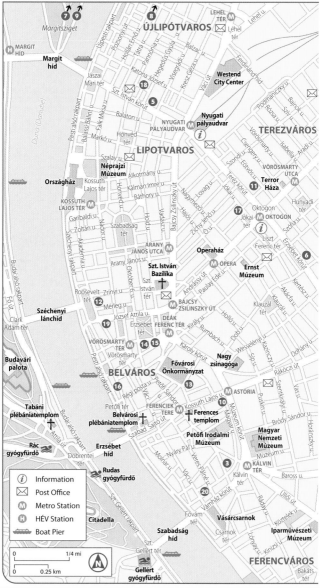

Andrássy Hotel MaMaison **1**
Atrium Fashion Hotel **2**
Best Western Hotel Art **3**
Boscolo New York Palace **4**
City Panzió Ring **5**
Corinthia Grand Royal Hotel **6**
Danubius Grand Hotel Margitsziget **7**
Danubius Health Spa Resort Helia **8**
Danubius Health Spa Resort Margitsziget **9**
Danubius Hotel Astoria **10**
Easy Hotel **11**
Four Seasons Hotel Gresham Palace **12**
Gerlóczy Rooms Deluxe **13**
Kempinski Hotel Corvinus **14**
Le Méridien Budapest **15**
Marriot **16**
Medosz **17**
NH Hotel **18**
Sofitel Budapest Maria Dorottya **19**
Zara Boutique Hotel **20**

Budapest Lodging **A to Z**

★★ Andrássy Hotel MaMaison PEST
Stylish Art Deco hotel with all the mod cons and designer furniture to match. Close to Heroes Square and houses fusion cuisine benchmark Baraka (see p 103). *Andrássy út 111.* ☎ *1/462-2100. www.andrassyhotel.com. 70 units. Doubles 105–395€. Breakfast 20€. AE, DC, MC, V. Metro: M1 to Bajza utca or H_sök tere. Map p 138.*

★ Atrium Fashion Hotel PEST
'Fashion hotel' with a striking central atrium and minimalist bijou rooms. The neighborhood is not the most salubrious but it is lively and central. *Csokonai utca 14.* ☎ *1/299-0777. www.atriumhotelbudapest.com. 57 units. Doubles 108–135€ w/breakfast. AE, DC, MC, V. Metro: M3 to Blaha Lujza tér. Map p 138.*

★ Art'otel BUDA
Chic with a lovely Buda riverside setting plus easy access to the Castle District and Pest, and great views to the Chain Bridge and Parliament. Art by Donald Sultan. *Bem rakpart 16–19.* ☎ *1/487-9487. www.artotel.hu. 164 units. Doubles 198–318€ w/breakfast. AE, DC, MC, V. Metro: M3 to Batthány tér. Map p 137.*

kids Beatrix Panzió BUDA
Clean and simple with a bit of a 70s retro hangover, Beatrix has a relaxing homely atmosphere. Self-catering 'Mediterranean' apartments are also available. *Széher út 3.* ☎ *1/275-0550. www.beatrixhotel.hu. 22 units. Doubles 60–100€ w/breakfast. No credit cards. Tram: 18/56 to Kelemen László utca. Map p 137.*

★ Best Western Hotel Art PEST
Tucked away in a charming and laidback narrow street just a step away from the action, the Art Deco columns recall this building's arty past while the modern rooms are spotless. *Király Pál utca 12.* ☎ *1/266-2170. www.bwhotelart.hu. 32 units. Doubles 90–180€ w/breakfast. AE, DC, MC, V. Metro: M3 to Kálvin tér. Map p 138.*

★★★ Boscolo New York Palace PEST
Seriously sumptuous from the moment you walk in to the modern but classically influenced Italianate lobby. Also houses the legendary New York Coffee

The sumptuous Boscolo New York Palace.

House (see p 35). *Erzsébet körút 9–11.* ☎ *1/886-6111. www. boscolohotels.com. 107 units. Doubles 169–509€ w/breakfast. AE, DC, MC, V. Metro: M3 Blaha Lujza tér. Map p 138.*

★ **Carlton Budapest** CASTLE DISTRICT Great location on a steep quiet street at the foot of the Castle District close to the Danube and Chain Bridge. Immaculate but small-ish rooms. *Apor Péter utca 3.* ☎ *1/224-0999. www.carltonhotel.hu. 95 units. Doubles 85–110€ w/break-fast. AE, DC, MC, V. Metro: M2 to Batthány tér. Map p 137.*

Citadella Hotel BUDA Basic hotel with five-star views over the river to most of Pest and much of Buda from where the Austrian occu-piers used to keep watch over the Magyars below. *Citadella sétány.* ☎ *1/466-5794. www.citadella.hu. 12 units. Doubles 46–51€ without breakfast. Breakfast 5€. Bus: 27 to Búsuló Juhász (Citadella). Map p 137.*

City Panzió Ring PEST Clean, comfortable, reasonably priced, and on major Pest thoroughfare close to Margaret Island. A bit noisy overlook-ing the street but brighter than the facing courtyard. *Szent István körút 22.* ☎ *1/340-5450 or 1/340-4884. www.taverna.hu. 39 units. Doubles 76€ w/breakfast. AE, MC, V. Metro: M2 to Nyugati pu. Tram: 4/6 to Nyugati pu. Map p 138.*

★★★ **Corinthia Grand Royal Hotel** PEST Behind the beautifully restored Habsburg period façade lies a seriously swish interior that brilliantly combines the best of old and new. The swanky rooms, awe-some atrium, grand ballroom, and spa facilities are a treat. *Erzsébet körút 43–49.* ☎ *1/479-4000. www. corinthia.hu. www.corinthiahotels. com. 414 units. Doubles 155€ with-out breakfast/350€ w/breakfast.*

Old world charm at Danubius Hotel Astoria.

AE, DC, MC, V. Metro: M1 to Okto-gon. Map p 138.

★★ **Danubius Grand Hotel Margitsziget** MARGARET ISLAND This handsome old-world riverside building is handily connected to the spa and sporting facilities of its sportier-looking Margaret Island twin by tunnel. *Margitsziget.* ☎ *1/889-4752. www.danubius group.com/grandhotel. 164 units. Doubles 137–180€ w/breakfast. AE, DC, MC, V. Bus: 26 to Szállodák (Hotels). Map p 138.*

★ **Danubius Health Spa Resort Helia** PEST A particularly good option for business travelers and conference planners where, after a long day, guests can take advan-tage of the spa and wellness facilities. *Kárpát utca 62–64.* ☎ *1/889-5800. www.danubiusgroup.com/helia. 262 units. Doubles 104–214€ w/break-fast. AE, DC, MC, V. Metro: M3 to Dózsa György út. Map p 138.*

★★ **Danubius Health Spa Resort Margitsziget** MARGARET ISLAND Outstanding spa utilizing leafy Margaret Island's three ther-mal springs and top wellness facili-ties with classically furnished rooms

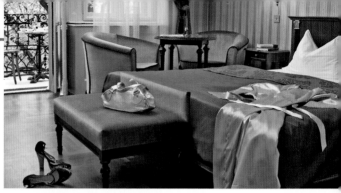

Elegant décor at Gerlóczy Rooms Deluxe.

in this now not so modern hotel. *Margitsziget.* ☎ *1/889-4700. www. danubiushotels.com/margitsziget. 267 units. Doubles 118–178€ without breakfast. AE, DC, MC, V. Bus: 26 to Szállodák (Hotels). Map p 138.*

★★ Danubius Hotel Astoria

PEST   Bastion of old-world charm in a very central location. Clean and comfortable with plenty of marble, elaborate carpets, crystal chandeliers, myriad mirrors, and stained-glass windows. *Kossuth Lajos utca 19–21.* ☎ *1/889-6000. www. danubiusgroup.com/astoria. 135 units. Doubles 90–214€ w/breakfast. AE, MC, V. Metro: M3 to Astoria. Map p 138.*

Four Seasons Hotel Gresham Palace Budapest.

★★ Danubius Hotel Gellért

BUDA   If you don't demand modern luxuries like air conditioning and free WiFi but value a unique lived-in atmosphere then this could be your place. Seriously eclectic. *Szent Gellért tér 1.* ☎ *1/889-5501. www. danubiusgroup.com/gellert. 234 units. Doubles 70–240€. AE, DC, MC, V. Tram: 18, 19, 47, 49 to Szent Gellért tér. Map p 137.*

Easy Hotel PEST   Bargain prices for clean, albeit orange, rooms in downtown Pest. Book online in the same way as budget air tickets whereby the cheaper rooms sell out first. Good choice for stag/ hen weekends. *Eötvös utca 25/a. www.easyhotel.com. 59 units. Doubles 29– 50€ without breakfast. Pay over the internet with all major credit cards. Tram: 4 or 6 to Oktogon. Map p 138.*

★★★ Four Seasons Hotel Gresham Palace Budapest PEST

Looking right onto the splendor of the Chain Bridge and with its stunningly restored Art Nouveau interior and rooms, outstanding service, breakfasts and spa, this is the place to splash out. The rooms keep an elegant but not over-stated Art Nouveau style. *Roosevelt tér 5–6.* ☎ *268 6000. www.fourseasons. com/budapest. Doubles 290–410€ w/breakfast. AE, DC, MC, V. Tram: 2* to Roosevelt tér. Bus: 16 to Roosevelt tér. Map p 138.

★★ Gerlóczy Rooms Deluxe

PEST Immaculate rooms elegantly furnished and true to the style of this charming 1892 building, which also houses the excellent Gerlóczy coffee house. It overlooks a charming and less discovered square. *Gerlóczy utca 1.* ☎ *1/501-4000. www. gerloczy.hu/roomsdelux/. 15 units. Doubles 85€ without breakfast. Breakfast 10€. AE, MC, V. Metro: M1/M2/M3 to Deák tér. Map p 138.*

★ Hotel Astra BUDA Spacious

rooms with antique furniture in a restored 300-year-old house. Spotlessly clean and comfortable, with an atmosphere that many guests say makes them feel at home. *Vám utca 6.* ☎ *1/214-1906. www.hotel astra.hu. 12 units. Doubles 99–112€. No credit cards. Metro: M2 to Batthyány tér. Map p 137.*

★ Hotel Panda BUDA Clean,

spacious, and colorful after a recent renovation, this Socialist-era hotel overlooks Bauhaus Pasaréti tér and has a forward-thinking policy of employing disabled people. Spa facilities. *Pasaréti út 133.* ☎ *1/394-1932. www.budapesthotelpanda.hu. 29 units. Doubles 70–100€ w/breakfast. AE, MC, V. Bus: 5 to Pasaréti tér. Map p 137.*

★★ Kempinski Hotel Corvinus

PEST The King of Budapest's luxury

Luxurious suite at the Lánchíd 19 design hotel.

Kempinski Hotel Corvinus.

hotels, until the Gresham Four Seasons and Corinthia Grand Royal came along to challenge its crown. Although starting to look a bit dated you can find some competitive prices by booking ahead. Nice spa facilities. *Erzsébet tér 7–8.* ☎ *1/429 3777. www.kempinski-budapest.com. 366 units. Doubles 129–299€ without breakfast, AE, DC, MC, V. Metro: M1/M2/M3 to Deák tér. Map p 138.*

★★★ Lánchíd 19 BUDA Seri-

ously chic designer hotel with close attention paid to detail and each room decorated with its own unique arty touches. Splash out on a suite, lie in the bath, and watch the Danube flow by. *Lánchíd utca 19–21.* ☎ *1/419-1900. www.lanchid19hotel.hu. 48 units. Doubles 162–240€. MC, V. Tram: 19 to Clark Ádám tér. Map p 137.*

★★ Le Méridien Budapest PEST

A deceptive river vista on its website taken in Buda aside, this classy and central hotel is big boutique rather than big chain and has a top French restaurant, Le Bourbon. *Erzsébet tér 9–10.* ☎ *1/429-5500. www.le meridien-budapest.com. 218 units. Doubles from 239€. Breakfast 25€. AE, DC, MC, V. Metro: M1, M2, M3 to Deák tér. Map p 138.*

★★ Marriott PEST Recently renovated from top to bottom with rooms kitted out with the mega-comfy Marriott Revive Bedding and views over the river to the Buda Palace to die for. Drink Bling deluxe water in the AQVA Lounge Bar. *Apáczai Csere János utca 4. ☎ 1/486 5000. www.marriott.com. 364 units. 119–225€, excluding taxes and breakfast. AE, DC, MC, V. Metro: M1 to Vörösmarty tér. Tram: 2 to Vigadó tér. Map p 138.*

Medosz PEST The building could be considered a Socialist period monstrosity but it's ideally located in downtown Pest, well priced, clean and comfortable, and just the place for someone looking to sleep behind the original 'iron curtain'. Surrounded by Pest nightlife. *Jókai tér 9. ☎ 1/374-3000. www. medoszhotel.hu. 67 units. Doubles 49–65€ w/breakfast. MC, V. Metro: M1 to Okogon. Tram: 4/6 to Oktogon. Map p 138.*

★★ NH Hotel PEST Stylish and exceedingly modern hotel tastefully tucked away behind the Vígszínház, the oldest theater in Budapest. Great breakfast. *Vígszínház utca 3. ☎ 1/814-0000. www.nh-hotels.com. Doubles 99–196€ without breakfast. AE, DC, V, MC. Metro: M2 Nuygati. Map p 138.*

★ Ramada Plaza ÓBUDA Luxury choice for business or pleasure on the banks of the Danube in Óbuda over the water from Margaret Island. Excellent thermal and wellness facilities on the site where the Romans once bathed. *Árpád fejedelem útja 94. ☎ 1/436-4100. 182 units. 120–2,000€ w/breakfast. AE, DC, MC, V . Suburban railway: HÉV to Árpád hid. Map p 137.*

★★ Sofitel Budapest Maria Dorottya PEST While new owner Accor couldn't change the Socialist-era exterior, the French hotel group

Uhu Villa offers a quiet retreat within the city limits.

has transformed the interior with expertly applied modern touches including a funky airplane in the striking lobby. Top Danube views. *Roosevelt tér 2. ☎ 1/2661234. www.sofitel.com. 350 units. 94–350€ double, 2,500€ suite, excluding taxes and breakfast. AE, DC, MC, V. Metro: M1 to Vörösmarty tér. Map p 138.*

★ Uhu Villa BUDA Cozy, friendly, and tastefully decorated with its own swimming pool, Uhu offers peace and quiet within the city limits. Most love it but a few gripe about its hilltop location, 10 minutes on foot from the nearest tram stop. *Kesely utca 1/a. ☎ 1/275-1002. www.uhuvilla.hu. 12 units. Rooms from 49€. AE, MC, V. Tram: 18/56 to Akadémia. Map p 138.*

★★ Zara Boutique Hotel Minimalism nicely executed with no expense spared on furnishings, Zara is a cool option in this enjoyable part of downtown Pest. *Só utca 6. ☎ 1/357-6170. www.zarahotels. com. 74 units. Doubles 105–230€ w/breakfast. AE, MC, V. Metro: M3 to Kálvin tér. Map p 138. ●*

The Danube Bend

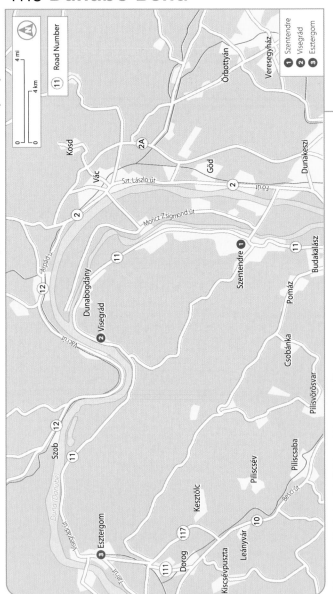

Road Number

11 Road Number

1 Szentendre
2 Visegrád
3 Esztergom

One of the prettiest stretches of the entire length of the Danube is blessed with three towns steeped in history, each of which I describe here. You could, at a push, see all three in one day, but a more manageable approach might involve Szentendre on one day and Visegrád and Esztergom together on another. From Szentendre it's 22km/13.5 miles by road to Visegrad from where it's another 24km/15 miles to Esztergom. START: **Batthány tér to take HÉV suburban train to Szentendre; or Árpád híd bus station in Pest for Visegrád; or Pest's Nuygati station for Esztergom.**

① ★★★ **Szentendre.** Of all the easy short hops from Budapest, Szentendre packs in the most history and color. The town is well on the tourist radar and attracts large numbers of visitors on a yearly basis. The inhabitants of Szentendre are well used to this, however; indeed, foreigners were flocking here centuries before the age of mass tourism, especially the Serbs who settled in the town en masse in the 17th century. I like walking around the beautiful cobbled Baroque main streets that run off the main square and then losing the tourist hordes by exploring the steep, narrow streets. Also, a walk along the

The colourful town of Szentendre.

Danube is a must and a look at the Belgrade Orthodox Church, with its adjoining Serbian Orthodox Museum, is a poignant reminder of Hungary's neighbors' influence on the town. ⏱ *½–1 day. Szentendre Tourist Information Office, Dumtsa J. utca 22.* ☎ *26/317-965. www. szentendre.extra.hu. Last stop on HÉV suburban train that starts at Batthány tér (approx. 40 min).*

② ★★★ **Visegrád.** The smallest town in Hungary is towered over by an imposing medieval citadel, which along with the lower castle was originally built by Béla IV in the 13th century to keep out the Mongols. The Royal Palace dates from the 14th century when Charles Robert of Anjou moved the Royal Court here. ⏱ *3–4 hr. www.visegrad.hu. Bus: from Szentendre or Árpád híd bus station in Pest.*

③ ★★★ **Esztergom.** Though the center of the Hungarian Catholic Church, Esztergom has a remarkable number of bars, and in this easy-going riverside border town, like most frontier posts, there's no shortage of opportunities to have fun. The biggest church in Hungary is situated on St. Thomas Hill, opposite what must be one of Hungary's smallest. Climb up the hill and stare over to Slovakia or walk over the bridge and enjoy some fine Slovakian draught beer. ⏱ *3–4 hr. Bus: from Visegrád. Train: direct from Pest's Nyugati station.*

A Wine Country Detour

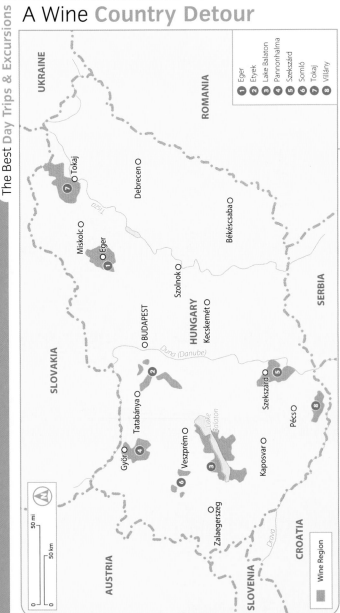

1 Eger
2 Etyek
3 Lake Balaton
4 Pannonhalma
5 Szekszárd
6 Somló
7 Tokaj
8 Villány

UKRAINE

ROMANIA

SLOVAKIA

SERBIA

HUNGARY

AUSTRIA

SLOVENIA

CROATIA

Tokaj 7

Miskolc

Eger 1

Debrecen

Békéscsaba

Szolnok

BUDAPEST

Kecskemét

Duna (Danube)

Tisza

Etyek 2

Tatabánya

Szekszárd 5

Győr

Pannonhalma 4

Veszprém

Lake Balaton

Somló 6

Szekszárd

Pécs

Villány 8

Kaposvar

Zalaegerszeg

Dráva

50 mi

50 km

0

Wine Region

Hungary's wines are one of its best-kept secrets and its wine regions are an engaging blend of rustic charm and state-of-the-art new wineries. You can increasingly turn up at wineries without invitation, but it's probably still best to call them beforehand. While you can reach anywhere in Hungary and get back the same day, it is worth staying over at most of its wine regions, especially since Hungary has a zero-tolerance alcohol policy and a car is the most convenient mode of transport. START: **All regions can also be reached by train or bus (check www.elvira.hu and www.volanbusz.hu respectively for timetables).**

① ★★★ **Eger.** The region famous for the generally lowly reputed mass-market Bull's Blood now has Bikavér Superior, a more refined, limited-yield version of the classic blend, as its flagship. The increasingly sophisticated Central European indigenous grape Kékfrankos forms the backbone of most Bikavér, but don't expect blockbusting full-bodied reds, as the beauty of Eger reds is their balance and finesse. With the climate comparable to Burgundy, it is no wonder that Pinot Noir features seriously. Also, a good region for whites—Monarchia winery (Verőszala u. 66, ☎ 0670/452-2626,

www.monarchiawinery.com) even lets you blend your own Bikavér. *140km/87 miles east of Budapest on E71/M3, taking E71/M3 then exit 114 and road 33.*

② **Etyek.** Etyek makes for a nice excursion in itself but its crispy whites are all the more reason to make the short 30km trip from Budapest for. Up on Öreg hegy, **Etyeki Kúria** (☎ 0630/9225-261) has mastered reductive fruity style Pinot Gris but also look out for its rustically elegant Királyleányka and delicious Sauvignon Blanc. It has also pioneered red wine in the

Wine growing around Lake Balaton.

region with its Pinot Noir that won the Best Pinot gong at 2008's Pannon National Wine Contest. *30km/18.65 miles west of Budapest on E60/M1, exiting at Biatorbágy.*

3 Lake Balaton. The shores and environs of the 'Hungarian Sea' present the Hungarian wine world in microcosm. The black volcanic basalt 'organ pipes' that rise up at Badacsony set the tone for the area's predominantly white mineral-infused wines. **Szeremley** wines put Badacsony on the path to renown and there is an excellent restaurant with sweeping views of the lake. *Saint Orbán Wine House Restaurant at Kisfaludy S. utca 5 in Badacsony. ☎ 87/431-382. www.szeremley.com. M7 to Balaton.*

4 Pannonhalma. Near the town of Győr, the Benedictine Monastery of Pannonhalma (Pannonhalma, Vár 1, ☎ 96/570-171, www.apatsagipinceszet.hu) is situated strikingly above a quant village. The UNESCO-listed monastery is well worth visiting in its own right and has its own state-of-the-art gravity-fed winery making very promising Tramini, Riesling, Pinot Noir, and a blockbuster fruit bomb of a red called Infusio. *133km/82.5 miles west of Budapest on E60/ M1–82.*

5 ★★ Szekszárd. Rapidly emerging from the big red shadow cast by Villány, Szekszárd is also doing well in international competitions with Bordeaux blends. The red Kadarka grape is a local specialty and can make delicious light but spicy reds. One of its finest proponents is the upcoming Bodri cellar (Vitéz utca 1, ☎ 0620/440-6666, www.bodribor.hu), whose wines are all good value in a region where the

prices of some of the best-known wines have become inflated. Unlike in Villány, wineries are far apart. *180km/112 miles south of Budapest. Take E73.*

6 ★★★ Somló. Hungary's smallest wine region is known for its fiery and spicy white wine. Even Britain's Queen Victoria loved it, especially when she heard about the propensity for women who imbibed wines made from Somló grape Juhfark (Sheep Tail) to mother male offspring. Sometimes, however, the wines are just too rough and acidic with too much mineral power. I suggest visiting the Kreinbacher winery (☎ 88/506-212), which has succeeded in making more polished, better balanced and fruitier wines that still have plenty of Somló. *164km/102 miles west of Budapest. Take E71 / M7 until exit 64 and connect with the E66 / 8 and head in the direction of and then past Veszprém to Somlóvásárhely where you will see Somló Hill.*

7 ★★★ Tokaj. Tokaj has the world's oldest wine classification system and its sumptuous elixirs were once the favorites of European royalty. Sun King Louis XIV dubbed Tokaji Aszú the 'King of Wines, and the Wine of Kings'. However, it's the winemaking that's happening now that makes this region so special. Hungary's one undeniably world-class region is blessed with its position at the confluence of the Bodrog and Tisza rivers. The mist that rises here enables 'noble rot' that concentrates the sweetness of wine. The region is also privileged with unique volcanic soils and a distinct portfolio of grapes in the form of Furmint and Hárslevelű. Since the fall of Communism, investment has piled in from those who know just how good this terroir is. The problem for Tokaj now is that sweet wine isn't the flavor of modern times. Yet the taste of one of these sublime elixirs, when made in the modern style, emphasizes freshness and sumptuous acidity, rather than overt sweetness. Also, less intense late-harvest styles and bone dry Furmints are gaining ground. Disznókő (at Mezőzombor, the Mád-Tarcal junction of the 37 road, ☎ 47/569-410, www.disznoko.hu) is one of the easiest to visit, and one of the best, as well as the first you'll encounter coming in from Budapest. *Tokaj town is 233km/144.8 miles northeast of Budapest. Take E71/M3—E71–E71/M30—E71/3 and take junction 37 to enter the region.*

❽ ★★★ **Villány.** Attila Gere whose blockbusting Bordeaux-style reds helped put Hungary's leading red wine region in the spotlight, both at home and to a certain extent abroad, has a large modern winery and visitor center at Erkel Ferenc utca 2/A, ☎ 72 492-839, www.gere.hu plus a cozy guesthouse in the village center at Diófás tér 4, ☎ 72 492-195. As it's a sign of the investment flowing into Villány that the Wunderlich winery (opposite the Gere winery) wouldn't look out of place in California—thankfully the winemaker is capable of making wines to match the grand ambition. While Cabernet Sauvignon and Merlot are good here, it's the lesser-known Bordeaux varietal Cabernet Franc that seems most at home and capable of unique expression. Local grape Portugieser makes enjoyable easy-drinking reds. Most of Villány's wineries can be accessed on foot, on and around the high street. *234km/145.5 miles south of Budapest. Take the same direction as Szekszárd, passing it and later taking road 57.*

Villány, Hungary's leading red wine region.

Lake **Balaton**

1 Balatonfüred
2 Tihany
3 Keszthely
4 Siófok

Kungós
Papkeszi
Balatonkarattya
Sóstó
Balatonvilágos
M7
Siófok **4**
Ságvár
Nagyberény
Bábonymegyer
Balatonszabadi
65
Som
Bótapuszta
72
Töreki
Lulla
Veszprém
Szabadság Puszta
Balatonalmádi
Balatonfüred **1**
Tihany **2**
Lovas
73
Kapoly
Nemesvámos
Kövesgyűpuszta
Balatonföldvár
Kereki
Pusztaszemes
71
Úrkút
Nagyvázsony
Balatonakali
Balatonszemes
Karád
Balaton
Ócs
Dörgicse
Révfülöp
Balatonboglár
Padragkút
Zánka
7
Szólóskislak
Somogytúr
Halimba
Kapolcs
Káptalantóti
Fonyód
Lengyeltóti
Hegyesd
Szentbékkálla
Nemesgulács
Badacsonytomaj
Csisztapuszta
Nyirád
Tapolca
Raposka
Badacsony
M7
Ödörögd
84
Nemesvita
71
Balatonmáriafürdő
Uzsa
7
Rezi
Keszthely **3**
71

0   8 mi
0   8 km

71   Road Number

The oft dubbed 'Hungarian Sea' is circled by a range of varied attractions and is much more than a place to go sailing with the in crowd or bask on its banks. These contrasting towns will give you an essence of Balaton and are best enjoyed over a few days touring. START: **The east tip of Balaton and all of these destinations can be reached in as little as an hour by car from Budapest on the M7 highway and most places here can be reached within two hours but allow extra time in peak periods. Trains depart regularly from Budapest's Déli station (for an interactive timetable go to www.elvira.hu).**

❶ ★★ **Balatonfüred.** The biggest resort town on the northern shore has an elegant old-world-cum-best-of-Communism feel, at least in parts, which is surviving well alongside the modern hotel developments. I enjoy walking around the waterfront, stopping for some deep-fried fish. The water is deeper here on the northern side and better suited to serious swimming. *Balatonfüred Tourist Information Office, Kisfaludy utca 1.* ☎ *87/580-480. www.balatonfured.hu.*

Lake Balaton.

❷ ★★★ **Tihany.** This pretty peninsula town is just 4km/2.5 miles from Balatonfüred. The narrowest point of the lake is topped off by the epic twin-towered Benedictine Abbey that hangs dramatically over the lake. It features an eerie crypt where you can read the engravings on the tomb of András, Hungary's very first King of that name, buried here in 1060. He also founded the still-functioning Abbey. *Tihany Tourist Information Office, Kossuth utca 20.* ☎ *87/448-804. www.tihany.hu.*

❸ ★★★ **Keszthely.** A rare pearl of Baroque beauty after countless repetitive resorts, Keszthely is home to the Festetics Palace. The abode of charitable counts, they built a hospital and the world's first agricultural university, the latter now being part of the University of Pannonia. *Keszthely Tourist Information Office, Kossuth utca 28.* ☎ *83/314-144. www.keszthely.hu.*

❹ **Siófok.** This is the undisputed party capital of Balaton, but it also has some pleasant beaches away from the action. The southern side has a very shallow shelf around waist height, which makes the water warm. Accessible from Budapest by Inter City trains it takes around two hours and much less by car if you drive as fast as a Hungarian. *Siófok Tourist Information Office, Viztorony (Water Tower).* ☎ *84/315-355. www.siofoktourism.com.*

Pécs

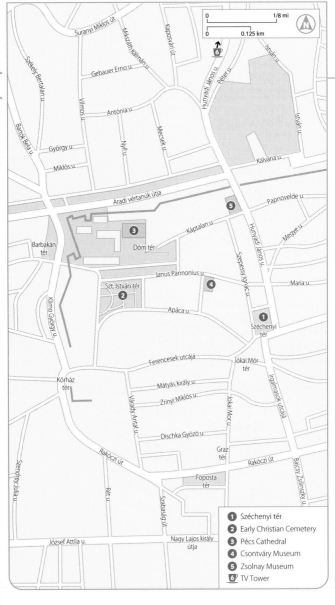

1 Széchenyi tér
2 Early Christian Cemetery
3 Pécs Cathedral
4 Csontváry Museum
5 Zsolnay Museum
6 TV Tower

Pécs is often touted as the Hungarian town with a mellow Mediterranean vibe, but you can also feel an influence from the Eastern Mediterranean Muslim world. All that's missing really is the sea. A day trip to this joint European City of Culture (2010) can be enjoyed on foot with all the attractions within close proximity to each other, except for the TV Tower. START: **Train from Déli pályaudvar (Southern train station), Budapest then head to Széchenyi tér.**

1 kids **★★★ Széchenyi tér.** This sloping and striking old town central square displays in its architecture some of the most significant periods in the city's history. The Church of Saint Mary in Turkish times was the Mosque of Pasha Gazi Kasim and still has a praying niche toward Mecca. Below it there's a Baroque holy statue, plus Baroque buildings all around, and a remarkable Art Nouveau Zsolnay fountain. ⏱ *45 min. Széchenyi tér.*

2 **★★★ Early Christian Cemetery.** A short walk away, this UNESCO-listed series of 4th-century

The town Hall on Széchenyi tér.

underground burial chambers features lavish murals depicting Christian themes and memorial chapels above ground. ⏱ *45 min. Szent István tér.*

3 **★★ Pécs Cathedral.** Impressive neo-Romanesque cathedral with four spires and elaborate frescoes from local and international artists throughout. ⏱ *45 min. Dóm tér.* ☎ *72/513-030.*

4 **★★★ Csontváry Museum.** Csontváry is my favorite of Hungarian artists, particularly for his originality and ability to breathe new life into tired themes. This comprehensive collection of his works is housed in a lovely museum. ⏱ *1 hr. Janus Pannonius utca 11.* ☎ *72/310-554.*

5 **★★ Zsolnay Museum.** The tiles that adorn many of Budapest's finest buildings like St. Matthias Church (see p 62) and the Applied Arts Museum (see p 15) hail from Pécs. If you're a fan then don't miss the collection at this museum. ⏱ *45 min. Káptalan utca 2.* ☎ *72/514-040.*

6 **★ TV Tower.** Hike up the 537m-high Misina peak and take the lift up to the 75m lookout tower that stands on top of it for breathtaking views. Its glass-walled café will transport you back to a 1970s spy movie. ⏱ *2 hr. Misina tető.* ☎ *72/336-900. Ft 600. Open 9am–9/10pm in season.*

Eger

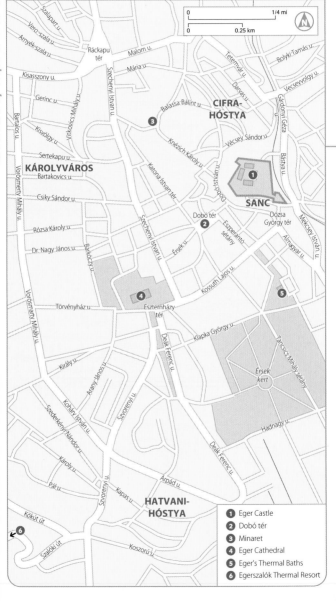

0   1/4 mi
0   0.25 km

Szalapart u.
Vero-szala u.
Arnyék-szala u.
Ráckapu tér
Malom u.
Kisasszony u.
Mária u.
Gerinc u.
Vitkovics Mihály u.
Balassa Bálint u.
Tetemvár u.
Darvas u.
Bolyki Tamás u.
Vecsevölgy u.
Gárdonyi Géza
CIFRA-HÓSTYA
Kisvölgy u.
Bartalos u.
Szechényi István u.
Knézich Károly u.
Vécsey Sándor u.
Sertekapu u.
KÁROLYVÁROS
Bartakovics u.
Katona István tér
Dobó István u.
Bánya u.
❶
SANC
Csiky Sándor u.
Vörösmarty Mihály u.
Rózsa Károly u.
Szechényi István u.
Dobó tér
❷
Esperanto sétány
Dózsa György tér
Almagyar u.
Mekcsey István u.
Dr. Nagy János u.
Bartóczky u.
Érsek u.
Kossuth Lajos u.
❺
Törvényház u.
❹
Eszterházy tér
Klapka György u.
Tancsics Mihály sétány
Vörösmarty Mihály u.
Király u.
Arany János u.
Szvorenyi u.
Deák Ferenc u.
Érsek kert
Szederkényi Nándor u.
Koltán István u.
Károly u.
Pál u.
Hadnagy u.
Kökút út
Arpád u.
Kapás u.
Maklári u.
Szoros u.
HATVANI-HÓSTYA
Deák Ferenc u.
Szalóki út
Koszorú u.
❻

❶	Eger Castle
❷	Dobó tér
❸	Minaret
❹	Eger Cathedral
❺	Eger's Thermal Baths
❻	Egerszalók Thermal Resort

Eger, together with its castle, is an iconic symbol of Hungarian defiance when the 'Stars of Eger' successfully repelled a mammoth Turkish force in 1552, after Budapest fell in the 1540s. Although the Turks took the town 44 years later in 1596 eventually, when the Ottomans were safely dispatched back to Istanbul after 91 years in 1687, Eger rebuilt itself at the height of the Baroque period and the result is stunning, making for a sensational walking tour. All of the sights on this tour, except the Egerszalók thermal bathing complex, are within close proximity of each other. For more information contact the Eger Tourist Information Office at Bajcsy-Zsilinsky utca 9, ☎ (06) 36/517-715. START: **Train from Keleti pályaudvar (Eastern railway station), Budapest then head to Eger Castle.**

① kids ★★★ **Eger Castle.** According to legend, the brave defenders of Eger Castle were fuelled by Bulls Blood, Eger's red wine, during the five-week siege in 1552. Consisting of just 2,000 Magyars, and led by István Dobó, they held off Ottoman forces 40 times their size. The Turks apparently thought the heroic Hungarians were imbibing the real blood of bulls. The effects of the wine wore off by 1596 as Eger Castle fell, and so ensued a 91-year period of Ottoman rule. Meet the stars of the battle in the István Dobó Museum within the Castle grounds. You'll also find the tomb of Géza Gárdony, the author of *The Stars of Eger*, also known as the 'Eclipse of the Crescent Moon', which depicts the events of 1552, as well as a dungeon. ⏱ *1 hr.* ☎ *36/ 312-450. Admission Ft 1,200 inc. museum, Ft 600 excluding museum. Every day 8am–8pm May 1 to Aug 31, closing 7pm in Sep, Mar and earlier in off-season (5pm Nov 1–Feb 28).*

② kids ★★ **Dobó tér.** To this day Eger is a remarkably well-preserved tour de force in Baroque architecture. This is particularly evident in and around this central square that is divided in two by the trickle that is the River Eger and has the Castle rising above it. However, as with so many squares in Hungary, a Socialist-era monstrosity steps in to spoil the party. In this case it's more of a Baroque ball, and the impostor comes in the form of the mini shopping center opposite the handsome dual-spired Minorita Church. ⏱ *45 min. Dobó tér.*

③ ★★ **Minaret.** This minaret is a pointy reminder of Eger's Ottoman occupation. It was once one of many but is the only one to have survived, albeit with no mosque attached, and as such is the northernmost surviving monument from the Turkish invasion. Scale the twisting staircase of 100 steps for panoramic views of the town. ⏱ *45 min. Knézich utca 1. Admission Ft 200. Open from Apr 1 to Oct 31, Tues–Sun 10am–6pm.*

④ kids ★★ **Eger Cathedral.** Seat of Eger's bishopric and the second biggest church in Hungary, this József Hild-designed, neo-classical cathedral (1836) is notable for the army of Christian statues towering above the columns at the entrance and its three cupolas. It's home to the biggest church organ in

Eger.

Hungary, whose magnificent and earth-shattering tones can be heard at regular summer concerts or during services. ⏱ *45 min.*

5 kids ★★★ Eger's Thermal Baths. A vast bathing complex where you can spend long summer days without getting in the least bit bored. Everything's there from a 50m/164ft swimming pool to thermal pools that work against arthritis and rheumatism. There's even a thermal pond with a waterfall that you can take a plunge in, as well as pools, a 'Wellness House', a water castle and slides for the kids plus restaurant and cocktail bar. The complex is also open for evening bathing every Thursday, Friday, and Saturday from 7pm to 11pm. Petőfi tér 2. Entrance from the Archbishop's Garden—throughout the year, entrance from Petőfi tér in summer. ☎ *36/314-142. www.eger termal.hu. Admission Ft 1,250. 8:30am–7pm May 1–Sep 30. 9am–7pm Oct 1–Apr 30.*

6 kids Egerszalók Thermal Resort. Just 6km/3.7 miles outside Eger at Egerszalók, this wonderful modern bathing complex is home to 17 indoor and outdoor pools. The resort is built around the incredible natural feature of a white limestone and travertine hill that rises dramatically out of Hungary's green northern uplands. *Egerszalók. Forrás út 4. ☎ 36/688-500. www.egerszalok furdo.hu. Admission Ft 1,200 for 3 hr (deposit Ft 2,400). 10am–6pm Mon–Thurs. 10am–8pm Fri–Sun. Lido open every evening until 1am in summer. Buses heading to Verpelét and Gyöngyös stop in Egerszalók.* ●

Eger Cathedral.

The
Savvy Traveler

  Chain Bridge

 Szilágvi D Square Presbyteria

Buda Castle

Before You Go

Government Tourist Offices

For the US: Hungarian National Tourist Office, 350 Fifth Avenue, Suite 7107, New York, NY 10118, ☎: 212/695-1221, www.goto hungary.com.

For the UK and Ireland: No walk-in service but interested parties are served via the website www.gotohungary.co.uk and a 24-hour English-language hotline on 00800 36 000 000, with calls free from the UK.

Travelers from Canada and Australia are not served directly but can make enquiries through www.goto hungary.com or through Hungarian embassies.

The Best Time to Go

Budapest's peak season runs from May to September, but with July and August often verging on the oppressively hot. The city does, however, have a wealth of baths that are a godsend when temperatures soar. May, June, and early September are usually ideal temperature-wise. August is a major vacation month so be prepared to find a fair number of restaurants, bars, and shops shut. Budapest is a good all-year destination and despite its cold winters there are plenty of indoor activities, plus outdoor novelties like skating and shopping at a Christmas market. Hotel prices are significantly cheaper in the off-season and the city is less overrun with tourists, making a strong case for an off-peak visit.

Festivals & Special Events

SPRING. The **Budapest Spring Festival**, a bevy of high culture including opera, classical, chamber music, dance, jazz, theater, and crossover, takes place during the last two weeks of March. It has featured many prominent international guests as well as the cream of local talent. Contact: www.btf.hu. On the last weekend of the Spring Festival, the offbeat **Budapest Fringe Festival** is described by its organizers as one big talent show, with everything from punk bands to acrobats and belly dancers. The hip arts melting pot of Millenáris is among the main venues (p 131). Contact: Bernadett Gárdos (☎ 1/486-3326), gardos@ budapestfringe.com.

Film fanatics get square-eyed at the **Titanic Film Festival**, which runs for 10 days at the end of March or the beginning of April and shows many Hungarian and international films, often ahead of their release dates. It runs simultaneously in the magnificent Art Nouveau-influenced Uránia and the arthouse cinemas of Toldi, Vörösmarty, and the Örökmozgó Film Museum. Contact: Balázs Vízer (☎ 0620/551-4927]), film@titanicfilmfest.hu.

SUMMER. On the summer solstice, June 27 in 2009, **Múzeumok Éjszakája** (Night of the Museums) allows culture vultures to visit many of the city's museums until 2am at seriously discounted prices (e.g. Ft 1,200 in 2007), while special buses are laid on by the Budapest transport company, BKV, to whisk participants between the museums. Tickets can be purchased at museums and some BKV ticket booths. Contact: www. muzeumokejszakaja.hu.

Although the main concert season runs from late September to early June, the **Budafest Summer Festival** sees the classical concerts, opera, and ballet continue throughout July at Szent István Basilica, the Hilton Dominican Court, and on Margaret Island, with Klezmer and folk music also included. Contact: ☎ 1/332-4816, viparts@viparts.hu.

On weekends in the second half of June to the second half of August, look out for **'Summer on the Chain Bridge'**, with stages on both sides of the bridge, and plenty of craftspeople exhibiting their wares on and around the bridge (which is closed to traffic). Lots of festival bites to eat are available, including the classic Transylvanian hollow whirly pastry known as *kalács*, which you can witness being made.

Hungary's answer to the UK's Glastonbury and America's Lollapalooza, the **Sziget Festival** takes place for just under a week in mid-August on an island (Hajógyári-sziget) within the city limits, so there's no need to camp out. Tickets for the 6-day event cost Ft 37,500 and Ft 30,000 respectively for camping and non-camping tickets, and Ft 8,000 per day (at the time of writing). The festival has featured many big names from The Cure, Iggy Pop, The Killers to Iron Maiden and underground international acts and leading world music performers, as well as many local artists, even Hari Krishna bands. There are many other typical festival attractions such as bungee jumping and abseiling. You can take a ferry from downtown Pest right into the action. A record 385,000 visitors attended the 2008 event. Contact: info@sziget.hu.

On **St. Stephen's Day** on August 20, hordes of Hungarians take to the Danube banks between Margaret Bridge and Szabadság Bridge to watch a stunning firework display.

FALL. During the first week of September, the **Jewish Summer Festival** sees a variety of concerts, including those by Israeli pop stars, at key venues in the Jewish district with the stunning Great Synagogue, also known as Dohány utca Synagogue, at the center. Contact: ☎ 1/ 343-0420. www.jewishfestival.hu.

Just about anyone who is anyone in the world of Hungarian wine puts in an appearance at the **Budapest International Wine Festival** that occupies the Buda Palace's grounds from Wednesday to Sunday around the middle of September. Contact: ☎ 1/203-8507, www. aborfesztival.hu.

In October things get seriously abstract during the **Budapest Autumn Festival** with lots of cutting-edge performance art, modern dance, offbeat exhibitions, and all that jazz. Contact: Festival director Zsófia Zimányi. ☎ 1/486-3300. info@festivalcity.hu; http://bof.hu.

On All Saint's Day, November 1, Hungarians visit cemeteries to pay their respects to departed relatives. More beautiful than macabre, cemeteries are lit up with candles and Kerepesi Cemetery, also known as Fiumei Úti Sírkert, at Fiumei út 16 in District VIII is the most spectacular.

WINTER. Christmas is a quiet family affair with the main celebration on the evening of December 24, while everyone comes out to party for the New Year, some even starting before noon on New Year's Eve at the races at Kincsem Park (60km from Budapest).

The Weather

Hungary has a continental climate with hot summers and cold winters where temperatures often linger below freezing point. Summers are hot and long, occasionally uncomfortable, with temperatures often hitting the high 80–90F/30C as early as mid-June and sometimes staying there until mid-September. The changeover to cooler temperatures at the end of September or October can leave people wondering what's happened to fall, and vice versa to spring in May. However, like many other countries in the world these days, precise temperatures are increasingly difficult to predict as

The Savvy Traveler

AVERAGE TEMPERATURES

	JAN	FEB	MAR	APR	MAY	JUNE
Daily Temp. (°C)	-1	1	6	11	16	19
Daily Temp. (°F)	30	38	43	52	61	66

	JULY	AUG	SEPT	OCT	NOV	DEC
Daily Temp. (°C)	21	21	16	11	5	1
Daily Temp. (°F)	70	70	61	52	41	38

Source: www.topbudapest.org

the effects of climate change take hold. An extremely mild Mediterranean-type winter can be followed by a typically cold one

Useful Websites

- **www.budapestinfo.hu** is Budapest's official tourism website and includes information on events, key sights, and the city's baths.

- **www.festivalcity.hu** contains detailed information on the Spring, Autumn, Fringe, and Summer on the Chain Bridge festivals.

- **www.budapest.com** is the city's travel and commercial portal and has a hotel booking search engine that gives instant confirmation.

- **www.elvira.hu** is an interactive train timetable that's accessible in English.

- **www.bkv.hu** provides detailed information on the city's public transport system.

- **www.xpatloop.com, expatshungary.com & www.caboodle.hu** are English-language sites that provide lots of practical information concerning life in Hungary. The latter's sister gastronomic site **www.chew.hu** contains detailed information on Hungary's cuisine and the culinary scene.

- **www.bbj.hu, www.budapesttimes.hu & www.budapestsun.com** are the main English-language newspapers and also come in print form.

Cell Phones

If your phone has GSM capability, then your mobile will work in Budapest. Roaming rates within the European Union have been cut drastically by regulators, making it much cheaper to use your phone in Hungary. Check with your operator before you leave. **www.apartmentsinbudapest.com** rents out mobile phones for 39€ per booking, not per day, with 80 free outgoing local minutes.

Car Rentals

With public transport still connecting the four corners of the city with relative ease, it is unlikely that you will need to rent a car. A rented car does come in handy though if you're looking to make excursions beyond the city limits. Prices are generally cheaper if you book online before you arrive in Budapest. **Fox Autorent** (www.fox-autorent.com) is a renowned local independent rental firm, while the likes of **AVIS** (www.avis.com) and **HERTZ** (www.hertz.com) have offices at the airport and across the city.

Getting **There**

By Plane
Budapest has one major airport, Ferihegy, which is located 15km/9.3 miles from downtown and divided into Terminal 1 and 2, with the latter subsequently split into Terminal 2A and 2B. Terminal 1 is mainly used by budget operators. The 200E bus connects both terminals and runs to Kőbánya-Kispest metro station where you can catch a metro to the downtown. Zóna Taxi (☎ 1/365-5555, www.zonataxi.eu) operates a reliable taxi service for Ft 3,600 to Ft 4,400 one way, the price depending on which of their zones your final destination lies in. Purchase taxi vouchers at the designated Zóna booths that you'll find directly outside the terminals. The Airport Shuttle (☎ 1/296-8555, www.airportshuttle.hu) mini bus service also runs from both terminals and the booking desks are located close to arrivals. A single ticket costs Ft 2,990 and a return is Ft 4,990. Book your return route no later than 24 hours before departure to ensure getting a return seat. Allow plenty of time for this option as other people are also being taken to their hotels and lodgings. On the return leg they pick you up at your accommodation.

By Car
All major Hungarian roads lead to Budapest and a car provides a useful way of getting to the Hungarian capital, although once in the city the driver will have the busy traffic and aggressive drivers to contend with. Try to enter or exit the city outside of rush hour (7am to 9pm and 4:30pm to 6:30pm) and you'll cut significant time off your journey.

By Train
Budapest has three main stations, which are named after the directions they originally served and to some extent still do. As well as Eastern destinations Keleti (Eastern) also handles most trains to Prague and Vienna. The other two are Nuygati (Western) and Déli (Southern), with trains from the latter going to Lake Balaton as well as Ljubljana and Zagreb.

By Bus
Budapest's new modern bus station is slightly out of the center at Népliget but it is connected to the metro system. Eurolines arrives and departs from here.

Getting **Around**

By Public Transportation
Budapest's public transport system efficiently links all corners of the city and its coverage is dense. It may be getting a bit creaky and dated, as it hasn't changed radically since the 1970s when it was considered a benchmark of Socialist planning, although newer buses and trams are being rolled out continuously. All parts of the city are covered in detail, whether it be by metro, tram, trolley-bus, or bus. Single tickets (Ft 290) or a book of 10 for Ft 2,600 can usually be bought at booths next to the bus stop or station, but it's advisable to stock up. Specific ticket kiosks at metro stations sell a wide

range of tickets and passes. Validate tickets at the top of the escalators before you get on the metro and as you get on trams and buses. One-day, three-day and seven-day travelcards that provide unlimited travel cost Ft 1,500, Ft 3,700 and Ft 4,400 respectively, although you need to provide a passport-sized photo for the latter. There is also the option of buying a family ticket for Ft 2,100. This will give 48 hours unlimited travel for 1 or 2 adults with 1 to 7 children between the ages of 6 and 14.

On Foot

Much of the center can be covered on foot and this is also the best way of seeing beyond the city's key sights, which is where much of Budapest's charm lies. On foot you can appreciate the scale of the early 20th-century building phenomenon that gave Budapest its defining look.

By Taxi

Taxis are abundant and are usually cheaper when you call one as opposed to flagging them down. However, the operators of many taxi firms don't speak English. Rates vary between operators but these three listed companies provide very competitive rates: City Taxi (☎ 1/211-1111), Tele5Taxi (☎ 1/555-5555), FŐTaxi (☎ 1/222-2222).

By Car

Hungarians love to drive and usually aggressively at that. Consequently, with the roads so busy and the actions of the local driver unpredictable, driving around the center can be a headache to say the least and is only for those who love the thrill of city driving in a new environment. Parking spaces are often hard to come by. Parking tickets are required in many central zones and are bought from coin-operated machines.

Fast **Facts**

APARTMENT RENTALS Dunahouse (www.dunahouse.hu) offers many apartments for rent (and sale) and has a huge network of offices across the city. IBUSZ (www.ibusz.hu) has a private accommodation service at Ferenciek tere 10 (☎ 1/485-2767), which provides a homely alternative to staying in a hotel as well as short-term rentals. Www.budarpads.com has shorter as well as long-term rentals.

ATMS/CASHPOINTS The easiest and most recommendable way to get cash in Budapest is to gain direct access to your account via one of the plethora of ATMs that offer MAESTRO, VISA and MASTERCARD and are now on most downtown streets. Although banks charge a

fee per withdrawal, it still remains the safest and best option as transactions are carried out according to a generally favorable wholesale exchange rate. At larger banks you can step in off the street to use the bank machines and security cameras are operated.

BABYSITTING Babysitter Training and Agency Center www.babaklub.com has a babysitter and au pair search function and uses only qualified babysitters, many of whom speak English. You can also use the search function for babysitters who speak English. The renowned Korompay Family Day Care at Menesi út 19 in District 11 (☎ 1/466-5740 or 0630/921-7820) also works in the English language and is run by former kindergarten teachers.

BANKING HOURS Most banks are open from Monday to Friday from 8am to 4pm, although some larger branches of major banks stay open until 5:30pm. Shops and hotels often cash travelers checks but at inferior rates to banks.

B&BS Local sites www.budapest hotels.com, www.justbookit.hu and the internationally popular www.tripadvisor.com provide online booking services for a wide range of Budapest hotels and often offer discounts compared to the regular prices you get when approaching a hotel direct. Tourist information portal www.budapest.com also has a hotel search and booking function.

BIKE RENTALS Budapestbike (www.budapestbike.hu) at Wesselényi utca 18 in District VII rents new Gepida Alboins for Ft 3,000 per day and tandems for Ft 5,000 per day with longer and shorter rentals also available. This enterprising company also arranges baths and pub tours.

BUSINESS HOURS Shops tend to be open from 10am to 6pm, although many stay open until 8pm in shopping malls.

CAR RENTALS Fox Autorent has offices at the airport, plus the Intercontinental and NH Hotels. See Car Rentals earlier in this chapter on p 162.

CUSTOMS Non-EU citizens over the age of 16 can bring in 250ml eau de cologne and 50g perfume, 200 cigarettes, or 50 cigars, or 250g tobacco, or a combination of these, up to 250g, while citizens from EU countries can bring in 800 cigarettes and much larger quantities of alcohol.

Non-EU citizens are allowed to enter with 1 litre of distilled alcohol and 2 litres of wine, while EU citizens are permitted to carry 90 litres of wine and 110 litres of beer into Hungary.

The same numbers apply when departing Hungary.

DENTISTS (see Emergencies, below).

DINING Eating out in Budapest is generally a casual affair with no jacket required except for a few exclusive restaurants (you should enquire when making a booking).

ELECTRICITY Like the rest of continental Europe, Hungary uses two-pin plugs and the 230V current. Adapters can be bought in electrical stores such as Media Markt.

EMBASSIES The Australian Embassy is at Királyhágó tér 8–9, District 12, ☎ 1/457 9777; the Embassy of Canada at Ganz utca 12–14, District 2, ☎ 1/392-3360; the UK Embassy at Harmincad utca 6, District 5, ☎ 1/266 2888; Ireland's Embassy at Gránit Torony in the Bank Center at Szabadság tér 7–9 ☎ 1/302-9600; and the US Embassy at Szabadság tér 12, ☎ 1/475 4400.

EMERGENCIES SOS Dental Service at Király uta 14 in District VI, ☎ 1/267-9602 and Stomatologia at Szentkirályi utca 40 in District VIII, ☎ 1/317-6600 offers around-the-clock dental treatment. Dial 104 for an ambulance.

EVENT LISTINGS www.funzine.hu has up-to-date information about cultural events, and look out for the print version free in hotels.

FAMILY TRAVEL The Budapest card is valid for one adult and one child up to 14 years of age costing Ft 6,500 and Ft 8,000 for 48 and 72 hours. It provides free travel and many sightseeing benefits, including free entry to numerous popular sights (see Passes).

GAY & LESBIAN TRAVELERS www.budapest.gayguide.net provides detailed information on accommodation, cruising, restaurants, saunas, events, etc.

Note: 2008's Gay Pride march was subject to vicious attacks from far right factions and as such it is uncertain whether it will continue in 2009. Despite this a lively gay scene has started to develop, although unsurprisingly many people in Hungary still choose to stay in the closet.

INSURANCE It is advisable to arrange travel insurance before departing your home country, although local private medical fees are reasonably priced. With its high standards for a low cost, Hungary is a serious health tourism destination, especially for dental care. For EU citizens emergency treatment is free on presenting a European Health Insurance Card (EHIC).

INTERNET ACCESS Internet cafes are increasingly common and you are likely to see them around downtown. Fougou at Wesselényi utca 57 in District VII (fougou.uw.hu, ☎ 1/787-4888) also does photocopying, printing, faxing, and scanning, from 7am to 2am. Www.hotspotter.hu, although in Hungarian, shows all wireless internet hotspots on a map with those marked in blue representing those that are free—click on the flag and the address comes up.

LIMOS Www.limohungary.com and www.onelimo.com handle suitably flash fleets.

LOST PROPERTY If your luggage is lost on arrival make a claim at the airport immediately. Police stations handle lost property. Check which district your items were lost or stolen in and go to that district's police station, although not much ends up returned.

MONEY Hungary uses the Forint (Ft or HUF). The exchange rate varies and at the time of writing $1 was worth Ft 181.5. Hungary is far from a cashless society and the use of credit cards is slowly catching on.

ORIENTATION TOURS City-Circle Sightseeing (☎ 1/327-6690, www.eurama.eu) runs a hop on/hop off city tour commencing every hour from the Chain Bridge and Hotel Intercontinental. Tickets cost Ft 4,500 and are valid for 24 hours.

Budapest vision (☎ 0630/9222-111 or 0670/617-4010, www.barbiebus.hu) operates 2-hr bus tours for Ft 4,000, 3-hr for Ft 6,000 and a hop on/hop off service for Ft 4,000, the latter including a 1-hr boat tour. Children up to 11 years old can ride for free. The meeting points are next to Deák tér in front of the Hotel Le Meridien or next to the entrance of Deák tér in front of the Evangelical Church on Erzsébet tér.

Cityrama (☎ 1/302-4382, www.cityrama.hu) runs a wide variety of tours in Budapest and beyond.

PASSES The Budapest Card costs Ft 6,500 and Ft 8,000 for 48 and 72 hours respectively. It's valid for one adult and one child up to 14 years of age and offers: unlimited travel on public transport; free or discounted entry to 60 museums and to several sights; reduced price tickets for cultural and folklore programs; discounts in restaurants, spas, and on car rental; travel accident insurance; and other benefits. It is available in 250 tourist and transport outlets across the city.

PASSPORTS Passports are issued by the relevant embassy who should also be contacted immediately in the case of lost or stolen passports. You are also required to report the incident to local police and request a a police report.

PHARMACIES Pharmacies are plentiful in Budapest and the one at Teréz körút 41 (☎ 1/311-4439) is open around the clock and charges a small fee for an after-hours service.

SAFETY Budapest feels remarkably safe at night compared to Western cities of a similar size, although isolated incidents do occur. Be wary of taxi drivers as even those of reputable firms have been known to rip off foreigners. Refuse to take a cab ride should they neglect to run the meter. Pickpockets can be a problem on public transport.

SENIOR TRAVELERS Foreign senior citizens are entitled to the same free public transport right as Hungarians.

SMOKING Many Hungarians smoke and Westerners are often shocked at how smoky many bars can be. Restaurants are required to have a non-smoking area and increasingly most do.

STAYING HEALTHY Ticks (*kullancs*) populate woodland areas in parts of Hungary, including the Buda Hills to some extent, and pose a threat in the form of Tick brain-inflaming Borne Encephalitis (TBE) and Lyme Disease. Cover up well in wooded areas and check for the little blood suckers later, especially behind your hair line. They can be twisted out with tweezers, but go straight to a doctor if the insect doesn't come out in one piece. Mosquitoes can be a pest in summer but don't carry malaria in Hungary. Insect repellent can deter both.

TAXES VAT (Value Added Tax) is known as ÁFA in Hungary and is charged and included on most goods and services at a rate of 20 per cent. VAT can be reclaimed at the airport on the purchase of goods.

TELEPHONES Cards can be bought at kiosks, while a few can be operated by coins of Ft 10, Ft 20, Ft 50, and Ft 100, although sometimes the coin slots are blocked by fraudsters.

The prefix for Budapest is 1, followed by a seven-digit number, but you drop the prefix when calling within the city. When calling Budapest from abroad, it is necessary to dial the country code for Hungary followed by the prefix and seven-digit number. When calling a Hungarian number beyond the capital, use the 06 prefix.

Mobile phones have more than 100 per cent penetration among the population and to dial a mobile you start with 06, followed by the prefix of one of the three providers: T-Mobile (30), Pannon (20), and Vodafone (70), which is subsequently followed by a seven-digit number. To call a Hungarian mobile from abroad, you start with the country code followed by the mobile provider's prefix and then the number.

TICKETS Central ticket offices supply tickets for the full gamut of concerts and performances. Jegymester (Bajcsy-Zsilinszky út 31, ☎ 1/302-4433, www.jegymester.hu), Ticket Express (Andrássy út 18, ☎ 0630/303-0999), Ticket Express Jókai utca (Jókai utca 40, ☎ 1/353-0692), and Vigadó Ticket Service (Vörösmarty tér 1, ☎ 1/317-6417).

TIPPING Adding between 10 and 15 per cent to restaurant and bar bills is the norm (be careful to check service hasn't already been added), but also for trips to hairdressers, beauticians, etc.

TOILETS Public toilets are not in great supply but can be found at the key transport hubs. You have to pay a small fee to use them, usually around Ft 100. Dropping into hotels discretely is often the best option.

TOURIST OFFICES The main tourist office is at Március 15 tér 7 (☎ 1/266-0479) with branches around town, such as Sütő utca 2 in District V next to Deák tér metro station and at all airport terminals.

TOURIST TRAPS Beware of service already being added to restaurant bills in some restaurants. If it is you needn't tip extra unless you were especially pleased with the service. Service charges are often mentioned on menus in English, but if not look out for the word *kiszolgálás*.

Avoid getting into unmarked taxis as they can really overcharge, and there have even been problems reported with reputable companies. Make sure the meter is running when you start your journey. The taxi driver will understand the word meter, if not the Hungarian word is *óra*—if you have problem rolling your Rs simply point.

The US Embassy carries a black list of rip-off joints to be avoided at all costs at: http://hungary.usembassy.gov/tourist_advisory.html.

TRAVELERS WITH DISABILITIES
Budapest is gradually waking up to the needs of disabled travelers but has a long way to go before it is on a par with Western countries. Getting on and off public transport can be a challenge, although the 4/6 trams that operate on the most important route can be accessed by wheelchairs as well as newer buses.

VAT See taxes.

Budapest: **A Brief History**

106 Roman Aquincum, now part of Budapest, becomes the center of lower Pannonia.

896 Seven Magyar tribes ride in to capture the Carpathian basin, including the territory known today as Hungary.

955 The Magyars are defeated at Augsburg, marking the end of their initial expansion into Western Europe.

1000 King István (Stephen) adopts Christianity leading to the Pope recognizing Hungary as a country.

1361 Buda becomes the capital of Hungary.

1541–1686 Turkish occupation.

1848 Ultimately unsuccessful Revolution against Habsburg rule.

1849 The Chain Bridge becomes the first permanent bridge between Buda and Pest.

1967 Reconciliation with Austria sees period of joint rule.

1873 Buda and Pest merge to become one city.

1920 The post-WW1 Treaty of Trianon sees Hungary lose some two-thirds of its territory.

1956 Revolution against Soviet-backed dictatorship sees the streets of Budapest become a battlefield with the Soviets returning to suppress the short period of freedom.

1970S Free-market reforms see Hungary become the 'happiest barracks in the [Warsaw Pact] camp'.

1989 A velvet revolution ensues after Hungary plays a major role in helping East Germans escape to the West.

2004 Hungary enters the EU on May 1.

2006 Riots ensue after a speech by Prime Minister Ferenc Gyurcsány at a closed party is leaked, in which he says his party screwed up their term of office.

Useful Phrases & Menu Terms

Useful Words & Phrases

ENGLISH	HUNGARIAN	PRONUNCIATION
Hello	**Jó napot!** (form.)/ **Szia!** (inf.)	*Your-nopot/ See-ya/*
Good morning	**Jó reggelt!**	*Your-reggelt*
Good afternoon	**Jó napot!**	*Your-nopot*
Good evening	**Jó estét!**	*Your-eshtate*
How are you?	**Hogy vagy?**	*Hodge-vodge*
Fine, thanks	**Jól, köszönöm!**	*Jol. cusunum*
Thank you	**Köszönöm!**	*Cusumum*
Good-bye	**Viszontlátásra!**(form.)/ **Szia!**(inf.)	*Visontlatasra*
Good night	**Jó éjszakát!**	*Yo ace-okat*
Yes	**Igen**	*Igen*
No	**Nem**	*Nem*
Excuse me	**Elnézést**	*Elnayzayst*
Sorry	**Bocsánat**	*Botch-arnot*
Do you speak English?	**Beszél angolul?**	*Besale ongolule*
Can you help me?	**Tudna segíteni?**	*Tude-na shegyteni*
Do you have...?	**Van...?**	*Von*
How much is it?	**Mennyibe kerül?**	*Men-yeeiber kerule*
When?	**Mikor?**	*Me-kore (me-core)*
What?	**Mi?**	*Me*
Give me	**Kérek**	*Kay-wreck*
Where is...?	**Hol van?**	*Hol-von*
the station	**az állomás**	*oz arllomash*
a post office	**egy posta**	*edge powsta*
a bank	**egy bank**	*edge bonk*
a hotel	**egy szálloda**	*edge sarl-odar*
a restaurant	**egy étterem**	*edge ate-erem*
a pharmacy	**egy gyógyszertár**	*george-sertar*
the toilet	**a WC**	*a vey-say*
To the right	**Jobbra**	*yobb-ro/a*
To the left	**Balra**	*bolra*
Straight ahead	**Egyenesen**	*edge-en-eshen*
I don't understand	**Nem értem**	*nem airtem*
What time is it?	**Mennyi az idő?**	*Men-yee oz idur*
I would like...	**Szeretnék...**	*Seret-nayke*
...to eat	**enni**	*any—**but** **emphasize and pronounce the double n**
...a room for one night	**egy szobát egy éjszakára**	*edge sobat edge ace-aka-ro*
...a taxi	**egy taxit**	*edge taxeet*

ENGLISH	HUNGARIAN	PRONUNCIATION
When?	Mikor?	*Me-kore (me-core)*
Yesterday	Tegnap	*Teg-nop*
Today	Ma	*Mo*
Tomorrow	Holnap	*Hol-nop*
Breakfast	Reggeli	*Regg-ily*
Lunch	Ebéd	*Ebade*
Dinner	Vacsora	*Votch-ore-a*

Numbers

NUMBER	HUNGARIAN	PRONUNCIATION
1	egy	*edge*
2	kettő	*kett-ure*
3	három	*har-um*
4	négy	*naydge*
5	öt	*urt*
6	hat	*hot*
7	hét	*hate*
8	nyolc	*knee-olce*
9	kilenc	*kee-lenc*
10	tíz (dyehth)	*tease*
11	tizenegy	*tease-en-edge*
12	tizenkettő	*tease-en-kett-ure*
13	tizenhárom	*tease-en-har-um*
14	tizennégy	*tease-en-naydge*
15	tizenöt	*tease-en-urt*
16	tizenhat	*tease-en-hot*
17	tizenhét	*tease-en-hate*
18	tizennyolc	*tease-en-knee-olce*
19	tizenkilenc	*tease-en-kee-lenc*
20	húsz	*huwse*
30	harminc	*har-mince*
40	negyven	*nedge-ven*
50	ötven	*urt-ven*
60	hatvan	*hot-von*
70	hetven	*het-ven*
80	nyolcvan	*knee-olce-von*
90	kilencven	*kee-lenc-ven*
100	száz	*saz*
1000	ezer	*ez-air*
2000	kétezer	*kate-ez-air*
3000	háromezer	*har-um ez-air*

Hungarian Menu

Most restauarants now have English-language menus but this list is useful in
the more basic places, and for translating the daily specials list which is
often Hungarian only.

HUNGARIAN	ENGLISH
Reggeli	Breakfast
Ebéd	Lunch
Vacsora	Dinner

HUNGARIAN	ENGLISH
Kenyér	Bread
Vaj	Butter
Méz	Honey
Dzsem	Jam
Sajt	Cheese
Sonka	Ham
Kolbász	Sausage
Tojás	Egg
Só	Salt
Bors	Peppers
Cukor	Sugar
Tej	Milk
Olaj	Oil
Ecet	Vinegar
Víz	Water
Ásványíz	Mineral water
Bor	Wine
Száraz	Dry
Édes	Sweet
Fehér	White
Vörös	Red
Sör	Beer
Pálinka	Fruit brandy
Husok	Meats
Bárány	Lamb
Csirke	Chicken
Kacsa	Duck
Liba	Goose
Marha	Beef
Nyúl	Rabbit
Pulyka	Turkey
Szarvas	Venison
Borjú	Veal
Comb	Leg
Mell	Breast
Máj	Liver
Sonka	Ham
Hal	Fish
Harcsa	Catfish
Kagyló	Mussles
Lazac	Salmon
Pisztráng	Trout
Rák	Crab, prawn
Ponty	Carp
Tonhal	Tuna
Burgonya	Potatoes
Hasábburgonya	French fries
Rízs	Rice
Tészta	Pasta
Zöldség	Vegetables
Gomba	Mushroom

HUNGARIAN	ENGLISH
Karfiol	Cauliflower
Kukorica	Maize
Lencse	Lentils
Sárgarépa	Carrot
Spárga	Asparagus
Spenót	Spinach
Hal	Fish
Zöldbab	Green beans
Borsó	Peas
Saláta	Lettuce
Uborka	Cucumber
Paradicsom	Tomato
Alma	Apple
Dinnye	Melon
Eper	Strawberry
Narancs	Orange
Őszibarack	Peach
Sárgabarack	Apricot
Szilva	Plum
Dió	Walnut
Gesztenye	Chestnut
Málna	Raspberry
Gulyásleves	Goulash soup
Bableves	Bean soup
Halászlé	Fish soup
Töltött káposzta	Stuffed cabbage
Hortobágyi palacsinta	Pancake with minced meat
Somlói galuska	Sponge cake with chocolate sauce, nuts, raisins and cream
Pörkölt	Stew
Harcsapaprikás	Catfish paprika with dumplings or pasta
Gundel palacsinta	Pancake with walnut, chocolate sauce and cream

Toll-free Numbers & Websites

AER LINGUS
☎ 800/474-7424 in the U.S
☎ 01/886-8844 in Ireland
www.aerlingus.com

AIR CANADA
☎ 888/247-2262
www.aircanada.ca

AIR FRANCE
☎ 800/237-2747 in
the U.S.
☎ 0820-820-820 in France
www.airfrance.com

AIR NEW ZEALAND
☎ 800/262-1234 or -2468
in the U.S.
☎ 800/663-5494 in
Canada
☎ 0800/737-000 in
New Zealand
www.airnewzealand.com

ALITALIA
☎ 800/223-5730 in
the U.S.
☎ 8488-65641 in Italy
www.alitalia.it

AMERICAN AIRLINES
☎ 800/433-7300
www.aa.com

AUSTRIAN AIRLINES
☎ 800/843-0002 in
the U.S.
☎ 43/(0)5-1789 in Austria
www.aua.com

BMI
No U.S. number
☎ 0870/6070-222 in
Britain
www.flybmi.com

BRITISH AIRWAYS
☎ 800/247-9297 in
the U.S.
☎ 0870/850-9-850 in
Britain
www.british-airways.com

CONTINENTAL AIRLINES
☎ 800/525-0280
www.continental.com

DELTA AIR LINES
☎ 800/221-1212
www.delta.com

EASYJET
No U.S. number
www.easyjet.com

IBERIA
☎ 800/772-4642 in
the U.S.
☎ 902/400-500 in Spain
www.iberia.com

ICELANDAIR
☎ 800/223-5500 in
the U.S.
☎ 354/50-50-100 in
Iceland
www.icelandair.is

KLM
☎ 800/374-7747 in
the U.S.
☎ 020/4-747-747 in the
Netherlands
www.klm.nl

LUFTHANSA
☎ 800/645-3880 in
the U.S.
☎ 49/(0)-180-5-838426
in Germany
www.lufthansa.com

NORTHWEST AIRLINES
☎ 800/225-2525
www.nwa.com

QANTAS
☎ 800/227-4500 in
the U.S.
☎ 612/131313 in
Australia
www.qantas.com

SCANDINAVIAN AIRLINES
☎ 800/221-2350 in
the U.S.
☎ 0070/727-727 in
Sweden
☎ 70/10-20-00 in Denmark
☎ 358/(0)20-386-000 in
Finland
☎ 815/200-400 in Norway
www.scandinavian.net

SWISS INTERNATIONAL AIRLINES
☎ 877/359-7947 in
the U.S.
☎ 0848/85-2000 in
Switzerland
www.swiss.com

UNITED AIRLINES
☎ 800/241-6522
www.united.com

US AIRWAYS
☎ 800/428-4322
www.usairways.com

VIRGIN ATLANTIC AIRWAYS
☎ 800/862-8621 in
continental U.S.
☎ 0870/380-2007 in
Britain
www.virgin-atlantic.com

Index

See also Accommodations and Restaurant indexes, below.

Photo **Credits**

Notes

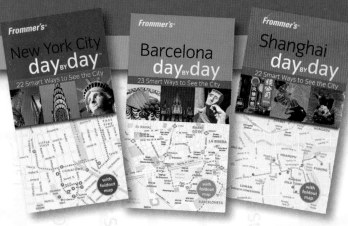